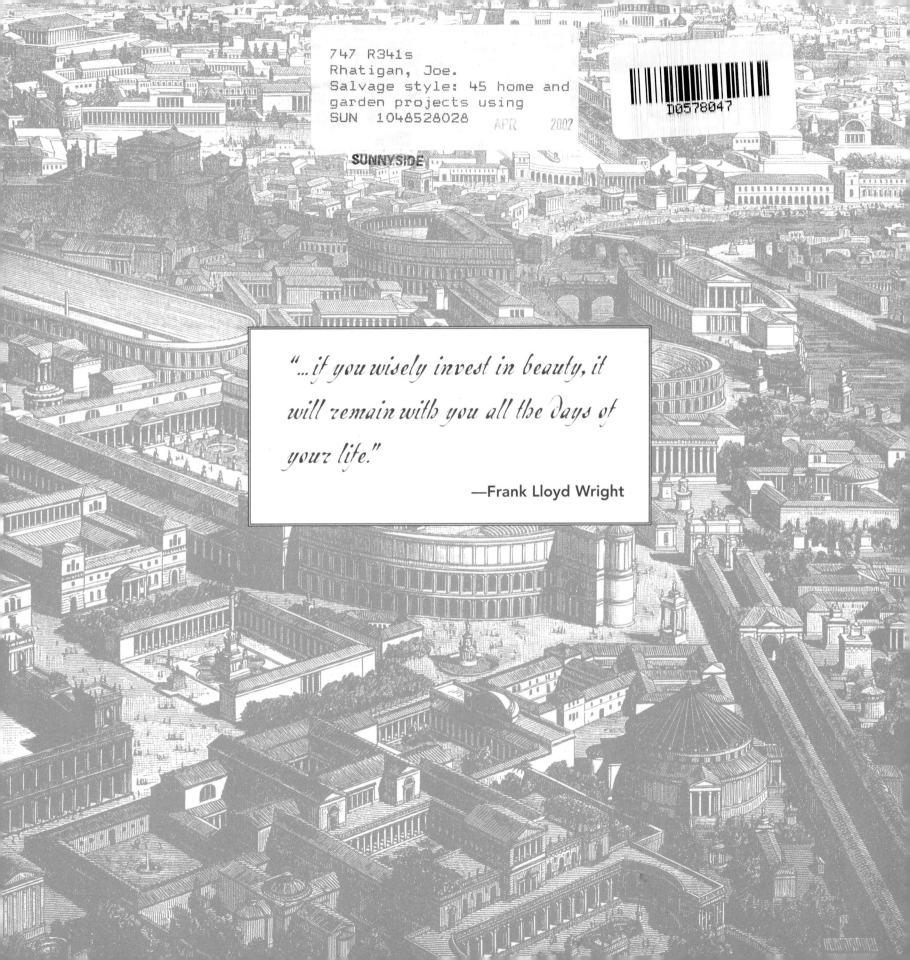

"...if you wisely invest in beauty, it
will remain with you all the days of
your life."

—Frank Lloyd Wright

SALVAGE *Style*

45

HOME
& GARDEN
PROJECTS
USING
RECLAIMED
ARCHITECTURAL
DETAILS

JOE RHATIGAN
WITH
DANA IRWIN

LARK BOOKS

A Division of Sterling Publishing Co., Inc.

Art director: **Dana Irwin**
Photography: **Sandra Stambaugh**
Illustrations: **Olivier Rollin**
Production assistant: **Hannes Charen**

Library of Congress Cataloging-in-Publication Data

Rhatigan, Joe.
        Salvage style : 45 home and garden projects using reclaimed architectural details / by Joe Rhatigan with Dana Irwin
        p. cm.
Includes index.
ISBN 1-57990-205-7 (alk. paper)
1. Handicraft. 2. House furnishings. 3.Architecture—Details.
4. Buildings—Salvaging. 5. Building materials—Recycling.
6. Building fittings—Recycling. 7. Found objects (Art) in interior decoration. I. Irwin, Dana. II. Title.

TT149 .R45 2000
747—dc21

        00-059506

10 9 8 7 6 5 4 3 2

Published by Lark Books, a division of Sterling Publishing Co., Inc.
387 Park Avenue South, New York, N.Y. 10016

© 2001, Lark Books

Distributed in Canada by Sterling Publishing,
c/o Canadian Manda Group, One Atlantic Ave., Suite 105
Toronto, Ontario, Canada M6K 3E7
Distributed in the U.K. by Guild of Master Craftsman
Publications Ltd., Castle Place, 166 High Street, Lewes, East Sussex, England
BN7 1XU
Tel: (+ 44) 1273 477374, Fax: (+ 44) 1273 478606, Email: pubs@thegmcgroup.com, Web: www.gmcpublications.com

Distributed in Australia by Capricorn Link (Australia) Pty Ltd., P.O. Box 704, Windsor, NSW 2756, Australia

If you have questions or comments about this book, please contact:
Lark Books
50 College St.
Asheville, NC 28801
(828) 253-0467

Printed in China

ISBN 1-57990-205-7

For Someone Like You...

TABLE OF CONTENTS

ED DOYLE, SELF-PROCLAIMED JUNKMAN

"Salvage lives!"

*A*n architectural detail is any piece removed from home or building that is in the process of being renovated or demolished. These details include doorknobs, flooring, mantels, windows, doors, etc., and the details that stand out are usually old, ornate, interesting, and weathered.

Salvage Style explores the creative, often remarkable, ways architectural details can be utilized in and around the home. Each of the 45 step-by-step projects uses a salvaged detail to create a new piece that serves a different function than the detail's original use. In other words, this isn't a book about how to replace your boring new doors with beautiful old doors, but instead, how to create a blanket chest out of an old basement door or a candleholder from a baluster.

Left: a spectacular view inside LASSCo, St. Michael's (The London Architectural Salvage and Supply Co. Ltd.), London's world-renowned architectural antiques shop, housed in a vast Victorian church

Right: This beautiful iron grate table was designed by J. Dabney Peeples, and served as the inspiration for the Garden Bench on page 84.

Each project has been designed to showcase the recycled item to its fullest potential, and in most cases, the project designers have retained the "look" of the salvaged detail, be it rusty, crusty, weathered, distressed, or paint-chipped. The skills needed for most of the projects are minimal, though experienced craftspeople will also find many interesting and challenging projects. And, even if you don't want to pick up a hammer, the projects can help inspire you to find that perfect look for your home.

DECONSTRUCTING HISTORY

*W*e study the past. We reshape, rewrite, romanticize, poke, and prod the past and call it history. When we take a bull-dozer to one of history's monuments, we cordon off the rubble like a crime scene. We dust for prints, find our own, and accuse ourselves of murder. Then we sift through what's left for mementos to lend us a fragment of a story we can relate, remember, and expand on—a narrative to replace all we have already lost....

Doorknobs
AND DIAMONDS

When I was a kid, I thought the glass doorknobs adorning every door of my family's 1920s bungalow were diamonds. I'd imagine how many baseball cards I could buy with just one of those doorknobs. When one popped off its spindle, I hid it under my pillow and wouldn't relinquish it until my dad convinced me it was glass. I believed him.

I believed him until I visited an architectural salvage warehouse in search of glass doorknobs to replace the ugly metal ones in my own 1920s bungalow. Just one of those doorknobs would have bought me an awful lot of baseball cards. A quick survey of the warehouse, along with a fair share of mental deconstruction, assured me that there was hidden value in most of the materials in my home. I sifted through the rows of peeling doors and well-worn mantels, the piles of flooring, and, of course, the doorknobs, and it

wasn't long before I was imagining the stories that went with each piece. I was surrounded by history deconstructed: pieces of architectural history under the rust and dust and grime of time and indifference. Out of context, these remnants may look like junk, but spend more than half an hour in a salvage warehouse, and you'll see these architectural details for what they truly are: the forgotten diamonds of our shared past.

Everything
AND THE KITCHEN SINK

Walking into a salvage warehouse or yard for the first time can be a mind-numbing experience. One part museum, one part junkyard, and one part antique shop, salvage warehouses offer an often chaotic display of reclaimed artifacts from demolished homes and buildings. In fact, at first glance, salvaged architectural details may seem like the poor first cousin (once removed) of shabby chic or rummage sale junk art. Look closer, however, and you'll find a thriving industry based on the simple premise of recycling reclaimed housing details.

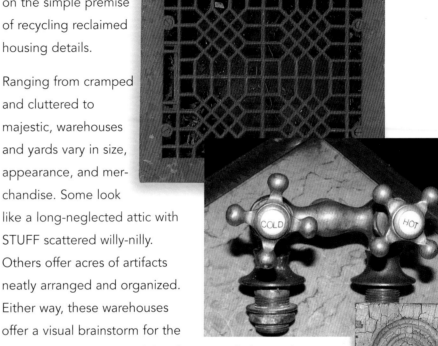

Ranging from cramped and cluttered to majestic, warehouses and yards vary in size, appearance, and merchandise. Some look like a long-neglected attic with STUFF scattered willy-nilly. Others offer acres of artifacts neatly arranged and organized. Either way, these warehouses offer a visual brainstorm for the seasoned seeker, even while often overwhelming the poor shopper simply searching for a matching doorknob.

Amidst the mounds of moldings, bricks, and brackets, you will usually find your local salvager. He or she may be known by many names: unbuilder, deconstructionalist, urban archeologist, reverse construction specialist, recycler, etc. But, by whatever moniker, today's salvagers truly act as history's gatekeeper—preserving what would have otherwise been destroyed.

For as long as people have carelessly demolished buildings, there have probably been a clever few standing by to nibble at the leftovers. As old homes and buildings succumb to highways and malls at an alarming rate, today's salvagers do more than merely nibble; they collect anything that can be removed from the building and reused. In fact, a salvage operation is usually all that stands between old homes and buildings and the landfill. Many salvagers do their own deconstructing, bidding on sites, and in certain circumstances, scurrying in just ahead of the wrecking ball and bulldozer to reclaim some worthy artifact.

Many salvagers have been in this business for years—long before recycling was a household term. In Europe, salvage attempts have been going on for hundreds of years. A lack of natural resources and a plethora of historically significant buildings led Europeans to salvage what couldn't be preserved a lot earlier than in North America. In North America, salvage yards began popping up in major cities in the 1960s, largely in response to urban renewal, when buildings were torn down to make way for massive new building projects. Entire neighborhoods were destroyed, and most of the building material ended up in landfills. The salvage yards that did exist reclaimed details primarily for remodeling purposes—finding a magnificently carved mantel from a demolished Victorian home to replace a boring new mantel. But it wasn't long before people were creating

exciting rooms and unique environments with decorative reclaimed elements—gardens decorated with chimney pots, and rooms sporting stone figures from an old building facade.

Today, architectural salvage is enjoying what could be called a prolonged fashion trend. "Vintage" replicas are for sale in catalogs, and the topic is featured in home improvement and decorating magazines and TV segments. Architectural elements are being used to create functional items that differ from the elements' original purposes. Many warehouses offer doorknob coatracks, pressed tin planters, salvaged wood furniture, etc., along with the raw materials to create your own projects.

The Thrill
OF THE HUNT

While wading through a salvage warehouse one day, I overheard the store manager ask a customer if she needed any help. "No, thanks," she replied. "Just looking for something that's looking for me." And, if you asked this salvage seeker why she spends hours at a time rummaging through old details, getting her clothes dirty, and coughing up 100-

year-old dust, she might reply that she admires the beauty of fine craftsmanship. Or, she might say that the antiquity of the pieces draws her in. She might even say she enjoys the satisfaction of knowing she is reclaiming pieces of the past her predecessors so carelessly threw away. But, if you've ever spent an afternoon with an avid salvage seeker, you know that gleam in her eye signifies the excitement of possibilities—the thrill of finding something unique and extraordinary and wonderful—that serendipitous moment when those hours of get-your-hands-dirty adventure pay off with a perfect fit: a decorative iron bracket that cries out, "We're meant for each other!" You can ask her what she's going to do with a decorative iron bracket, but she may not even understand the question. It doesn't matter. And even if she doesn't find anything that day, she still has the splinters in her hands to show for her efforts.

Then there's the guy who wants to build a table. He'll scour every inch of the warehouse picking up pieces and putting other pieces back, until he has a conglomeration of what a novice might call junk. But with just his vision and a couple of nails, that guy will have a one-of-a-kind table that was

created without cutting down any new trees and that didn't need to be shipped from anywhere in a big gas-guzzling truck.

Whether they put their architectural finds to decorative or practical use, today's salvage seekers come to satisfy their need for quality design and materials—the craftsmanship that's so evident in much of the salvaged architectural details, and so apparently missing from much of today's architecture. The only regret (and it's not really a regret) is that reclaiming architectural details used to be a well-guarded secret. Alas, no longer.

The Economics OF SALVAGE

Of course, the allure of reclaiming architectural details goes beyond the thrill of finding it. The economics of salvage have received more and more attention as communities seek to "go green" and adapt a more environmentally friendly attitude. Simply speaking, salvage saves money and resources. Usually when a house has outlived its usefulness, it's bulldozed and hauled to the nearest landfill. A good chunk of the cost of demolition is the fee the contractor pays to unload a dumpster at a landfill. That can

Below: The architecturologists of Olde Good Things (New York, NY) went to great heights to salvage a woman's head from the top of the Ellis Auditorium in Memphis, Tennessee before the building was demolished.

cost thousands of dollars. And, up to 20 percent of what is dumped in landfills today is construction waste. Deconstruction creates fewer trips to the landfill, saves perfectly good materials from being wasted, and eliminates the need for new materials, consequently discouraging the use of valued natural resources. Even a building that's dilapidated beyond repair is 50 percent reusable. Unfortunately, governments still don't understand the economics of architectural salvage. In many cases, salvagers have to deal with tons of paperwork, legal maneuvering, and insurance nightmares just to be allowed to enter a building about to be demolished. And even with the popularity of architectural salvage, most salvagers will agree that they are only reclaiming a portion of what's being demolished. Either through lack of interest, complicated legal obstructions, or simple laziness on the part of officials, administrators, contractors, home owners, and demolishers, too much of our past architectural history is being lost to landfills.

They Don't Make 'Em
LIKE THEY USED TO

It's an age-old truism, but it's apt. They don't make houses like they used to. And to tell you the truth, that's a good thing. Houses built prior to the 1970s are covered in lead-based paints that are known to present serious health risks. Balusters and railings were made wide enough so kids could get their heads stuck between them. Electrical fixtures are outdated. Old houses creak. They groan. The wind whips right through them. Old houses are not easy

places to get warm. New housing has corrected so many of the problems of the past. New houses are so much more suitable for living—they're safer and warmer...and oh, so sterile. Many old homes were built when lumber was of a higher quality and the standards of craftsmanship were higher. Today's cookie-cutter mentality is producing safer houses of much poorer quality. You could spend a million dollars on your perfect, modern, dream home and still feel like there is something missing. Where are the details that prove someone cared about how this house was built? Where are the stories? The real fascination behind reclaiming architectural details lies in the narratives each piece furnishes. Age confers dignity (the more rust the better), and antiquity provides the stories we fill our lives with. When the past is destroyed, we seek to recapture pieces of it to hang on our walls to transfer that dignity to ourselves. Each salvaged artifact provides something to grasp onto as we zip forward through the new century. A place to stop and ponder: who owned the house this came from? Why is the corner of this mantel chipped? How did that finial end up here? When you buy an architectural remnant, you are paying for a piece of history and its story (real or imagined). If you live in a new home, adding a few well-chosen salvaged details can bestow some originality, character, and flair.

The Future
OF SALVAGE

As long as we relish stories, there will be a need for architectural salvage warehouses to provide the missing narratives for our homes. Unfortunately, most salvagers agree

that there will not be much to salvage in, say, 50 years. More and more older buildings are being preserved (which is good!), and today's homes don't contain the same quality ornamental detail people crave. Simply speaking, the only thing that's going to be worth salvaging when today's homes succumb to the wrecking ball is the lumber. In fact, although today's lumber is vastly inferior to old-growth lumber, it will be superior to the lumber produced in the future. So, when the wrecking ball starts going after the homes being built today, the salvager of the future will be looking for the wood, as the cost of truly decorative, well-crafted remnants from the 18th, 19th, and early 20th centuries skyrockets and becomes something only the extremely well-off can afford.

Something Old...Something New: RECONSTRUCTING HISTORY

Today, when a historically significant building outlives its original purpose, architects often renovate it for new uses for the new owner, keeping the building viable and away from the wrecking ball. I work in a building that used to be an insurance office. I have three glass-paneled doors in my office (only one of which works), and I assume my office used to be a waiting room. The architects who renovated this building left the doors in place, preserving the building's ornate past while adapting it for the building's new life. This process is called adaptive reuse, and it applies just as importantly to architectural remnants. Many remnants

have outlived their original usefulness. Old windows are not as good as new windows. Sure they look better, but they were built during a time when heat was relatively inexpensive, so they don't do as good a job sealing out the elements. But just because a 75-year-old window doesn't make a good window anymore, that doesn't mean it can't still add warmth and detail to a room as a divider between open living and dining areas, for example. Adaptive reuse can apply to old automobile tires, plastic containers, or whatever, but rarely will you be able to achieve the elegance that is attained when using a well-crafted remnant from our architectural history. And years from now, who knows, that mantel you used as a headboard may be pried from the wall, and one salvager will say to the other, "This headboard will make a great mantel for our fireplace."

Above: A cherub in distress! The architecturologists of Olde Good Things rescued this amazing terra cotta cherub from the rubble of a hotel in Baltimore, Maryland that was in the process of being demolished. Below: This dolphin frieze was one of many salvaged from the Ellis Auditorium in Memphis, Tennessee by Olde Good Things.

Olde Good Things is New York City's premier architectural salvage storehouse that specializes in rare architectural finds. From ornate marble mantel pieces from Harlem brownstones to original advertisements off of a Times Square landmark, their inventory also includes over 10,000 doorknobs, 3,000 doors, and 300 mantels.

TIPS AND TECHNIQUES

Making something new out of something old can be as simple as nailing a mantel to a wall to create a headboard. Other times, however, a project may take some skill, planning, and know-how. The projects in this book were

designed primarily for people who love to recycle architectural fragments, no matter what their skill level. Almost every project can be completed by someone who has never used a power saw before. But that doesn't mean a power saw won't make life easier. There are projects that need some woodworking, welding, glass cutting, and other skills, but don't be put off if you don't possess them. This section provides essential information for working with wood, metal, and glass, including tools needed, safety precautions, and step-by-step techniques that will

help you in times of uncertainty. If you still feel uncomfortable with some of the techniques, seek help from a qualified professional. He or she can assist you with a couple of the steps you are uncertain about, or even work from a sketch or photograph you provide. Sometimes a call to a home improvement center is all you will need. For many people, the truly thrilling part of working with salvaged architectural details is actually finding that perfect piece of history to call their own, and then figuring out what to do with it. In other words, if you are not comfortable cutting your own glass for picture frames, buy pre-cut glass or have

a glass cutter do the job for you. Don't be afraid to learn, but also don't make things unnecessarily difficult for yourself. Shortcuts are good. This book is meant not only to inform and teach, but also (sometimes primarily) to inspire.

So, continue reading. In fact, read this section carefully. You won't find every answer to every question, but you will find the information you need to build your first several projects. Plus, it's good to know the lingo so you can speak knowledgeably to the people you are seeking help from.

What Else You Need
TO KNOW ABOUT THIS BOOK

As you've probably already noticed, unlike most books that include how-to projects, *Salvage Style* doesn't focus on one craft. In fact, some projects will have you cutting wood and then hammering some tin one step later.

Finally, it's important to note that, also unlike most how-to books, the instructions for the projects in *Salvage Style* do not necessarily include detailed measurements and dimensions. Why? Because the window you find for your Shutter and Window Showcase (see page 124) will not be the same size and shape as the one the designer of the project used. We all have different tastes, and a completely different window might be calling your name, demanding you use it not as a display for books, but for CDs! You can relax and take that window home, knowing that the instructions for the project you have in mind for that window have already taken personal taste and need into account. In many cases, the project instructions list materials to be sized according to the size of the recycled piece, giving you the freedom to experiment with variations. There is a lot of room for experimentation. Have fun!

A Note
ON MEASURING

In many of the projects included in this book, you will be measuring the architectural detail you have found for the project and measuring the

rest of the materials according to the detail's dimensions. In some cases you may wish to draw a diagram. Another useful method is to measure against the fit. In other words, hold the board to be cut against the place where the piece will fit, then adjust the measurements as necessary. However you end up measuring for the project, careful and accurate measurements will ensure the best possible results. So beyond the tape measure and the straightedge ruler, you may wish to purchase a *try square* and/or *combination square.* A try square consists of a metal blade placed at a right angle to a handle. You'll use this square to establish 90° angles for boxes and frames. It can also be used to mark cuts across the face of a board. Large try squares are called *framing squares.* A combination square consists of a cast handle fitted to a metal blade. The handle can be moved back and forth perpendicular to the blade and is designed in such a way that it can also form a 45° angle. The combination square does everything the try square does, and it also measures 45° angles and can act as a depth and miter gauge.

Use these tools to double-check your angles, frames, boxes, and cuts before moving forward. As the old adage goes, "Measure twice, cut once."

WORKING WITH WOOD

There are a lot of projects included that call for working with wood, and whether you're an experienced woodworker or a beginner, it would serve you well to read through this section. Working with wood is one thing, but working with old, weathered, nail-ridden wood is quite another thing entirely.

WOODWORKING TOOLS

For each project's tool list, great care has been taken to provide not only the most adequate tools for the job, but also the simplest. If a tool list calls for a handsaw, then a handsaw is perfectly fine for the job. However, if you have a power saw that can do the job more quickly and easily, then by all means use it.

Skimming through different projects' tool lists, you won't come across too many uncommon items. The hammers, screwdrivers, drills, and saws are all there. You can decide whether or not to go electric and use power tools. But, before beginning one of the woodworking projects, make sure you at least have the basics.

Smooth and level working surface: If you're working on an uneven basement floor, you won't be able to tell whether the legs on the table you're building are square and even. An old door without panels or a piece of thick plywood supported by sawhorses will work. Also make sure the surface is large enough to accommodate the project you're building.

Assorted flathead and Phillips screwdrivers

Hammers: You'll need a couple of hammers (large and small).

Nail set: This tool will help you countersink nail heads so they will sit below the surface of the wood.

Clamps: A variety of clamps is essential for woodworking. You'll use them not only to apply pressure and hold joints together until the glue sets, but also as valuable aids when assembling your projects. By using clamps, one person can assemble even a large project. When you apply clamps, always insert a piece of wood or a clamp pad between the clamp and your work. Without this cushion, your clamps may leave marks on the surface of the project. *C-clamps* are good for securing a piece of wood to a work surface. *Bar and pipe clamps* are used to hold assemblies together temporarily while you add the fasteners, as well as to apply pressure when boards are glued together edge-to-edge. *Web clamps* are used for clamping such things as chairs or drawers. They exert a uniform pressure completely around a project. *Spring clamps* are handheld clamps that are perfect for securing smaller items to the work surface, and also for exerting pressure until the glue dries.

Tape measure

Straightedge ruler

Try square or combination square

Handsaws (a combination saw or rip saw and crosscut saw): Though having a variety of power saws you know how to use is quite helpful.

Drill with assorted bits

Sanding block and sandpaper

Goggles

Dust mask

CUTTING WOOD

A piece of wood may be *ripped* (cut along its length) or *crosscut* (cut across its width). Specific saws or saw blades exist for each procedure. With a few exceptions, you can make all of the cuts necessary for the projects in this book with a handsaw. Just keep in mind that cutting with handsaws requires some extra time and patience.

The most popular power-cutting tool is the *circular saw*, the blade of which can be adjusted to cut at a 90° or 45° angle, or any angle in between. With a circular saw, you can use a combination blade that rips or crosscuts. Even though circular saws are heavy and can make for less-than-accurate cuts, a fence can be added to guide the saw to make the cuts more accurate. You'll need a rip fence for rip cutting.

A *coping saw* consists of a steel, U-shaped frame with a very thin, brittle blade fastened under tension across the U's opening. A handle is attached to the frame for ease of sawing. Use a coping saw to make curved and interior cuts on wood less than 2 inches (5.1 cm) thick.

A *backsaw* is often used to make smooth joinery cuts with the use of a *miter box*. The miter box is open at both ends, with slotted sides to guide a saw in cutting joints. Standard miter boxes are built for making 45° and 90° angle cuts.

A *jigsaw* is a power saw used to cut curves, shapes, and large holes in boards.

A couple of projects call for use of a *router*, which is a handheld power tool that can cut decorative shapes and round edges, create grooves and notches, and make joints. It can be difficult to operate, so practice on scrap wood before using a router on serious work.

Keep in mind that every saw will remove an amount of wood from the piece you're cutting equal to the thickness of its blade. This waste is called the saw's *kerf,* and you'll need to account for it whenever you make a cut. The kerf should always be on the waste side of the cutting line.

The projects in this book use simple methods of joining wood together. The following list defines and illustrates the most common joints used.

Butt Joints: This is a simple joint in which one board abuts another at a right angle (see illustration below). A butt joint must be reinforced with fasteners of some kind—usually screws.

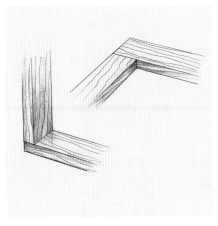

Dado Cuts and Joints: A dado is a slot or groove cut into the face of a board to accommodate the thickness of another board or other material (see illustration below). A dado may be cut with a handsaw and chisel, a router, or a dado set on a circular saw.

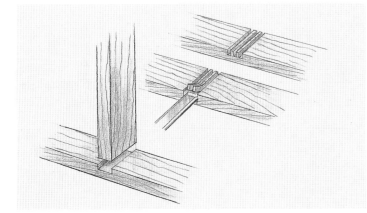

Miter Cuts and Joints: A miter is an angle, usually 45°, cut perpendicularly across the width of a board. Two mitered boards joined together create a right angle without exposing the end grain of either piece—providing a finished, all-wood corner appearance. Because glue does not hold end grains, miter joints are weak and must be reinforced with screws or nails.

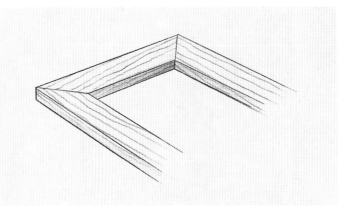

Mitering

Mitering molding and wood for frames is a relatively simple matter requiring nothing more than a miter box and a backsaw. Since a number of projects call for mitering, detailed instructions have been provided here. Simply refer to this section when the instructions for a project call for mitering.

Instructions

1. Place the piece of wood you are going to cut in the box, butted hard against the near side.

2. Place a piece of scrap wood under the wood to be cut so the saw can run through without damaging the bottom of the box.

3. Make sure the blade is aligned in the correct slots (45° angle in most cases). If you have already measured the piece to be cut for the project, make sure the saw cuts the angle without altering the measurement. To do this, position the wood so that the saw cuts the angle without cutting the outer edge. However, for best results, measure your pieces for the project after the first cut.

4. Hold the backsaw in one hand, with the index finger pointing along the blade, while the other hand firmly holds the wood to be cut. Make sure the wood stays put. If it moves or twists, then chances are the resulting joint won't fit.

5. Make the cut by first pulling the saw toward you for the first couple of strokes. Then push the saw to deepen the cut. Don't use too much force. Let the weight of the saw do most of the work. Use steady, smooth strokes.

You can also miter corners and full-length edges (to create boxes) with a circular saw or a compound miter saw.

FASTENING

When selecting fasteners, consider whether the project will be placed outdoors or indoors. If it's an outside project, choose screws and nails that can withstand the rigors of the elements. Galvanized steel nails and screws provide good weather resistance, though the more expensive stainless steel nails and screws will outlast them all. However, if you want the nails or screws to rust for a more consistent look, then the cheaper fasteners will work wonderfully. Select screws and nails that will penetrate the second thickness of wood as far as possible without coming through its opposite surface. Make sure that if you wish to countersink screws you are using the flat-head variety.

Driving nails at an angle, rather than straight in, produces an even tighter hold; this process is known as *toenailing*. With some practice you can do the same with screws.

Finally, although you don't want to add so many screws or nails to your project that the metal outweighs the wood, don't be stingy with them. If there's the slightest chance that a joint could be shaky, add a couple extra screws or nails.

PILOT HOLES

Drilling pilot holes for nails and screws prevents the wood from splitting, hence it is a good idea to drill pilot holes when dealing with old or decorative wood. For

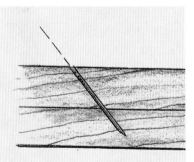

Toenailing

nails, drill the holes about two-thirds the length of the nail and slightly smaller in diameter. For screws, use successively sized drill bits to first create a pilot hole, which should be about half the diameter of the screw, and then a shank hole, which should be the same diameter as the screw's shank.

WOOD PLUGS AND COUNTERSINKS

The easiest way to cover screw and nail holes is to use wood filler, a colored plastic substance that hardens when exposed to air. Try to match the filler to the final color of the wood. Predrilling holes for countersunk screws is normally a two-step operation. First, a pilot hole is drilled. Then a larger, countersunk hole, slightly larger in diameter than the screw head, is centered and drilled over the pilot hole to accommodate the head of the screw. If you use the same size screws on a regular basis, you may wish to invest in a combination pilot-countersink bit for your drill, which will perform both operations at the same time.

The countersunk portion of the hole can be just deep enough to allow the head of the screw to sink below the wood surface, or it can be deep enough to accompany both the screw head and a wood plug inserted on top of the head. Wood plugs can be purchased or made by cutting off slices from a wooden dowel. Dip the plug in a small puddle of glue, start it into its hole, and tap it into place with a hammer. Allow the glue to dry, then trim it with a sharp chisel.

REMOVING NAILS

Many times, the architectural fragment you buy will still have the original nails sticking out

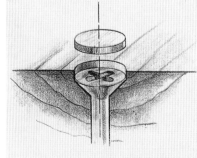

Countersink with wood plug

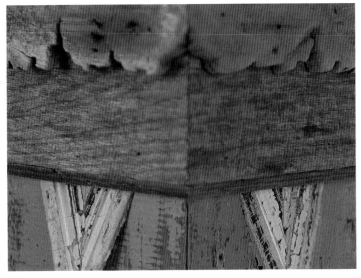

of it. And chances are the nails will be rusty. If the nail point is showing, but you can't find the head on the other side, your best bet is to cut the nail with a hacksaw. Locating the head may require digging it out of a countersink, and the process will mar the piece. If the nail is stubborn, and simply using a hammer claw is of no help, or if the nail head popped off, first, slip the hammer claw around the exposed nail shaft. Then tightly clamp a pair of locking pliers onto the nail as close as possible to the hammer claw. Pull back on the hammer handle until the nail starts to pull out. Stop, reposition the hammer claw and pliers farther down on the nail shaft, and repeat until the nail has been completely removed.

SANDING

Any project may be sanded by hand. An inexpensive plastic sanding block will do the job of sanding a level surface just fine. The amount of sanding required for each project depends on how you'll be using the project and the salvaged detail's "look." Since many of these projects depend on the detail that you find for it, sand the rest of the wood to match the look of the detail. Also, don't sand anything made before 1978 before reading about lead-based paints in the Safety Issues section (see page 25).

PROTECTION FROM THE ELEMENTS

You're going to want to protect your outdoor wooden projects from the elements (especially those wooden "gems" you've found at the salvage warehouse). Proper finishing can add years of enjoyment to your project, and since you've spent the extra money for a beautiful architectural detail, you probably won't want to paint it. For best results, use a simple coat of *clear sealer*. Often used to weatherproof decks and railings, most water sealers penetrate the surface of the wood and offer a high degree of protection. They range in appearance from muted and barely perceptible to smooth and semigloss sheens. Water sealers need to be reapplied every year. You can also use nearly translucent stains that contain a sealer.

WORKING WITH METAL

This section will not be as lengthy as the previous one for the simple fact that there are not as many metal projects, and there isn't enough room here to teach you how to weld. If you are interested in the few welding projects in this book (all relatively simple), and you can't weld, simply ask someone who can weld to do it for you. Show the welder your architectural detail and work from there. That's exactly what designer Dana Irwin did for her garden bench on page 84. She found the heat registers and showed them to a welder, who then worked from a simple design she sketched. Both were

incredibly satisfied with the results. Whatever you do, don't automatically dismiss the welding projects because you don't weld. Let the projects at least inspire you; decorative iron is beautiful, sturdy, and even, at times, majestic.

METALWORKING TOOLS

The tools for working with metal in this book depend largely on the metal piece you have found. In some cases, no tools will be needed at all. Other times, you may need to straighten out a bent portion of iron fencing, or drill screw holes into iron.

Tin snips or metal shears: You'll need a sharp pair of snips or shears to cut tin or copper sheeting.

Abrasive sponge: These sponges are used to smooth the edges and remove small burrs of cut tin or copper.

Wire brush: Use this brush to remove rust.

Flat file: Files are used to shape and finish the surface of metal.

Hammers: A heavy hammer is perfect for banging bent metal back into place.

Hacksaw: A hacksaw is the simplest tool to use to cut metal pieces such as iron fence rails, nails, etc.

Drill with assorted bits

Center punch or awl: Mark where holes will be cut or drilled in metal with these.

Gloves: Gloves are a must for working with tin.

Safety goggles: These are needed when rust is being removed from iron pieces, and when using power saws to cut metal.

Level

CUTTING TIN

Cutting tin is not a difficult process. Make sure you are wearing gloves and a long-sleeved shirt to lessen the chances of a scrape. Lay the tin on your work surface. Measure and mark the cut line, and carefully cut the tin with the snips. Each cut should end near the point of the snips. Once the tin is cut, you may have to flatten the edges. To do this,

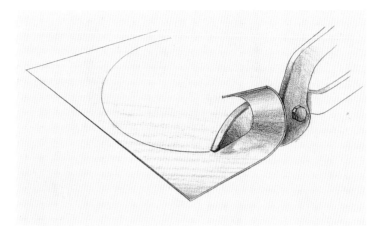

place a block of scrap wood over the edge, and hammer until the edge is flat.

DRILLING INTO METAL

An electric hand drill is used for drilling holes in metal, though if you have access to a drill press, use that instead. First, you should center punch the work where the hole will be drilled. Then, squirt a drop of oil into the center punch mark. Clamp the work securely and drill the hole.

BENDING METAL

To straighten out a bent piece of iron fencing or railing, start by securing the straight end of the piece in a vise as

close to the bend as possible. Then, if your work surface is stable enough, hammer the bent end until straight. Another method (for bigger pieces) is to place the piece on a solid, smooth surface with the bent piece sticking up, and hammer the bend until it is flush with the surface.

CUTTING OTHER METALS

Cutting metal with a hacksaw is easy. Clamp the work to your work space, and start the cut on the backstroke. Apply pressure only on the forward stroke. Once the cut is made, remove any burrs with a flat file or abrasive sponge.

CREATING THREADS

One of the easiest ways to attach doorknobs or faucet knobs to other surfaces is to use a tap to cut threads into the holes and then attach with bolts. Securely clamp the

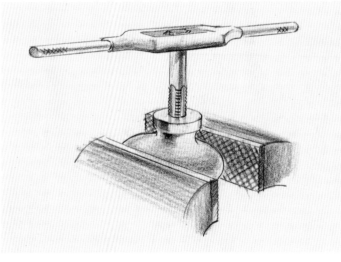

knob to your work surface, and find a tap that will screw into the hole. Place the end of the tap in the hole, and use a tap wrench to turn the tap clockwise with a small amount of downward pressure. To make sure the tap is going straight into the hole, remove the tap wrench and check the tap with a try square. Then, squirt a little oil into the hole before placing the tap back into the hole. Resume turning until the threading is complete.

WORKING WITH GLASS

$\mathscr{W}$hether you are working on an old window or creating a frame for a mirror, this section will take you through the basics of cutting, removing, and replacing glass and mirror.

TOOLS FOR BREAKING, CUTTING, AND REPLACING GLASS

Straightedge ruler

Crayon or grease pencil

Glass cutter: This is an inexpensive tool that scores the break line in the glass. Some have built-in oil reservoirs to provide automatic wet cuts.

Kerosine or sewing machine oil: You can use either to lubricate the wheel of the glass cutter.

Glass-cutting pliers: These pliers offer an alternative method for breaking a scored piece of glass.

Putty knife

Chisel

Pliers

Gloves

Safety goggles

CUTTING GLASS

Cutting your own glass is a skill well worth honing. The most important thing to remember is that cutting glass involves two major steps: *etching*, or *scoring*, a line in the glass, and then cleanly breaking the glass along the score line.

You'll need a smooth, flat surface to work on. Cover the surface with a piece of heavy cardboard (glass has a nasty habit of breaking when you don't want it to).

Instructions

1. Using the crayon or grease pencil and ruler, draw your cutting lines on the glass. Make use of the existing outer edges of the glass whenever possible.

2. Hold the ruler along the line to be cut and place the glass cutter alongside it, perpendicular to the glass. Oil the cutter with kerosine or sewing machine oil before cutting (a dry cutter creates a ragged, chipped score line).

3. Start in about ⅛ inch (3 mm) from the edge of the glass. Using firm pressure, pull the cutter toward yourself with one slow, continuous stroke. Use a little less pressure as you end your stroke. Do not stop and start. Remember, you are simply trying to score the glass, not cut it.

4. Place the scored glass along the edge of the table. Match up the scored line with the sharp edge of the table, keeping the scored side up.

5. Keep the glass on the table weighted down with one hand. With your other hand, hold the overhanging glass firmly. Raise it just slightly off the table, then snap it against the table edge. You can also use a pair of glass-cutting pliers to cut the glass. Hold the glass firmly on one side of the scored line. Hold the pliers in your other hand with the flat side on top. Open the pliers and grasp the glass near the scored line. Bend the pliers downward.

6. Run the toothed part of your cutter around the cut edges to get rid of any shards.

7. If your glass doesn't cut, don't run the glass cutter back over a scored line. Instead, tap along the score line with the rounded end of the glass cutter and try to break it again.

REMOVING A PANE OF GLASS FROM A WOODEN WINDOW FRAME

If you're not interested in saving the glass from the window, simply place the window in a large, plastic garbage bag, and hammer the glass out. Then, remove the window frame from the bag, and use pliers to remove any remaining shards of glass and glazier points. With a screwdriver or chisel, scrape away any remaining caulking. If, on the other hand, you would like to save the glass, use a flat-head screwdriver or chisel to remove the old glaze or caulk. Use the pliers to remove glazier points. Pick out the glass from the frame.

REPLACING BROKEN WINDOW GLASS

Glass is usually held in place by a fastener, and then putty or a glazing compound is applied to keep out the rain.

Instructions

1. Carefully remove all pieces of glass with pliers.

2. Remove the old caulking. As you proceed around the frame you will find glaziers points (small steel triangles). Remove and save them.

3. With sandpaper, clean off bits of putty that remain on the wood.

4. Measure the size of the glass, and reduce each measured dimension by ¼ inch (6 mm).

5. Buy glass cut to fit, or cut the glass to the correct size yourself.

6. Put a thin ribbon of glazing compound or putty in the groove on the frame for the glass to rest on. Keep the thickness of this glazing compound fairly uniform, so when you press the glass down onto the compound it will not crack.

7. Install the glass. Press it onto the glazing compound, and insert the salvaged glazier points with a large screwdriver. The points should be placed every 6 to 8 inches (15.2 to 20.3 cm).

8. Knead the glazing compound and form it into strings no bigger than a pencil.

9. Lay a string of compound along one side at a time and force it onto the glass and wood frame with the tip of a putty knife. Remove smudges later on with a turpentine-dipped cloth.

SAFETY ISSUES

As with any craft involving tools, safety should always be a primary concern. Along with the standard safety advice about wearing protective eye gear, working with architectural details involves other safety issues. Many architectural details were painted with lead-based paints, now known to be quite hazardous to one's health, plus many details will be rusty or will contain rusty nails. Please read this section before moving on. This is important stuff.

GENERAL SAFETY

■ Wear safety glasses or goggles whenever you make a cut or drill a hole.

■ Protect your lungs with a dust mask. Even a cheap dust mask will filter out most of the harmful particles that result from cutting, sanding, or drilling.

■ Wear earplugs when operating power tools.

■ Wear close-fitting, comfortable clothes. Fast-moving blades can catch on loose clothing.

■ Keep a first-aid kit next to your work space.

■ Wear rubber gloves when working with solvent-based liquids.

■ Wear gloves and goggles when working with glass.

■ Don't lean over glass as you cut it. A slip could cut you.

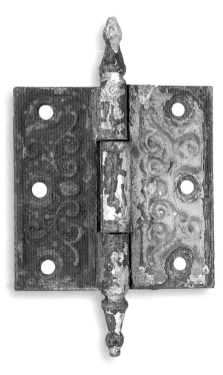

or not to leave it as it is or seal it. If children will have access to the object, then by all means, remove it or seal it. You may also wish to pay a responsible professional to strip it off-site. I don't recommend stripping lead paint yourself unless you know how to dispose of the resulting waste material according to governmental guidelines. The best way to deal with lead paint is to seal it or paint it. If you wish to keep the piece with the same distressed finish you found it in, use a clear polyurethane finish to seal the piece, preventing the paint from flaking and falling. You can wash the surface with a surfactant, such as trisodium phosphate, which loosens dirt and removes lead dust prior to painting.

SAFETY ISSUES WITH ARCHITECTURAL DETAILS

▪ Update your tetanus shot. Working with rusty nails and tin, you are bound to get a cut sooner or later. You know the old saying, "an ounce of prevention...."

▪ Don't cut into an old piece of wood until you have checked for nails within the wood. Hitting a nail with a circular saw could send the blade flying. Use a stud finder to locate hidden nails.

▪ Finally, dread lead. Lead-based paint, a toxic material, was widely used on both the exteriors and interiors of buildings until the second half of the 20th century. When lead paint deteriorates, it chips and produces dust particles that are a known health hazard. Children are especially at risk when they ingest lead paint dust through direct contact and from chewing lead-painted surfaces. If you are planning on stripping an architectural detail, have it tested for lead first. Lead-testing kits are available at home improvement centers. If it tests positive, you must decide whether

TO CLEAN OR NOT TO CLEAN

*B*esides washing your architectural details with mild soap and water, you will probably not wish to strip the surface of its original finish. Removing the patina or original finish diminishes the allure of the piece; so if possible, get rid of the dirt but little else. Sometimes, you may want to get rid of some of the paint (after testing for lead). How thoroughly you clean and strip is a matter of personal taste, though, once again, the point remains to clean it minimally. When cleaning a piece, make sure you are outside or in a well-ventilated area. Place the piece to be cleaned over a plastic drop cloth to catch the debris, and don't forget to wear gloves and a mask. Use a wire brush, cloth, sandpaper, or whatever you need to get rid of the dirt and the paint you wish to remove, but not the character. For some pieces, compressed air or a ball of tape may remove all the dust and residue necessary. Once done, fold up the drop cloth and dispose of appropriately.

When dealing with rusty iron, you will have to remove the rust with a wire brush before welding or repairing it. And since a lot of old iron looks wonderful newly painted, you may wish to completely refurbish it. If so, clean the piece thoroughly before continuing. Test the paint for lead before moving forward.

A little rust goes a long way on this fanciful umbrella stand fashioned out of salvaged decorative iron.

JUST ONE MORE WORD OR TWO
BEFORE YOU GET STARTED

You've probably already checked out the projects and found some you'd like to get started on, but before you run out to salvage hunt, take a few more minutes to narrow your choices. If you're new to the art of salvage hunting, you may wish to start with something small and easy, such as the Rosette Clock on page 32 or You've Got Mail on page 98. If you are not a woodworker, don't begin with the Old Door Futon Sofa (on page 73) or the Pedestal (on page 118). They are not extremely difficult projects, but they are time consuming and require some more advanced tools. Also, take a look at the materials and tools for the projects. Will you need to buy or rent a tool? Do you need lumber? And most importantly, will you be able to locate an architectural detail for the project? The best bet may be to search out the salvage warehouses in your area to see what they have in stock. See page 69 for a comprehensive list of ways to find salvaged architectural details.

Also, decide what type of lumber you will use for the projects. Some of the projects in this book call for old barn wood, which is easier to find in some areas than others. If you can't find barn wood, some other type of salvaged wood may suffice. Or would you rather use regular stock from a lumber yard? Also, remember that the instructions are written for basic tools. If you have more advanced tools, adjust the procedures accordingly.

Finally, remember to be safe and have fun. If you're new to salvaging architectural details, let this book get you started on a lifetime adventure that will change the way you look at your house, garden, and neighborhood. If you're already hooked, you may find some projects you've attempted already, but I think you will also be surprised by the resourcefulness and ingenuity of the designers and their projects.

THE PROJECTS

"If you foolishly ignore beauty, you'll soon find yourself without it. Your life will be impoverished. But if you wisely invest in beauty, it will remain with you all the days of your life."

—Frank Lloyd Wright

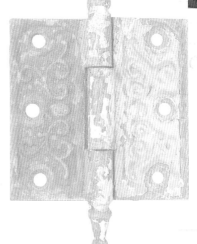

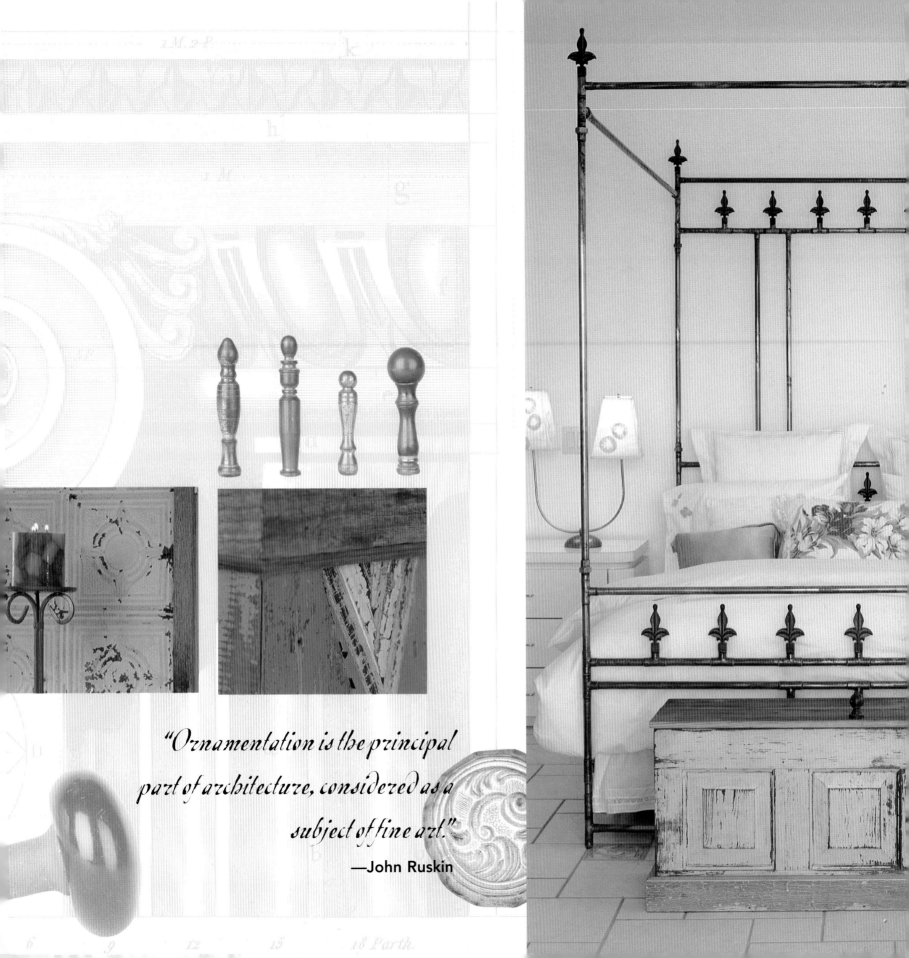

"Ornamentation is the principal part of architecture, considered as a subject of fine art."

—John Ruskin

MANTEL HEADBOARD

*M*antels make great headboards, and whether your tastes run toward elaborate Victorian scrollwork or angular art deco, there's a mantel out there for you. Not only does the perfectly chosen mantel confer instant dignity to your bedroom, but it also provides a classy place to lay your book after some late-night reading.

INSTRUCTIONS

1 Place the mantel where you wish it to go.

2 Put the bed in the center of the opening, and make sure you are completely satisfied with the mantel's location.

3 If you wish to secure the mantel to the wall, locate the studs, and since the mantel will probably cross at least two studs, hammer nails into the mantel wherever it lines up with a stud.

4 Use the nail set to countersink the nail heads.

Another way to secure the mantel is to use hanging brackets (also sometimes known as mantel brackets). One set of the brackets attaches to the wall and the other to the back of the mantel. Some hardware stores and home improvement centers carry them.

DESIGNERS
JOYCE YARLING & ROGER LEICHTER

MATERIALS

Old mantel

Bed

Long finish nails (optional)

TOOLS

Stud finder (optional)

Hammer

Nail set

ROSETTE DESK CLOCK

*R*osettes are decorative moldings used to connect the side trim and head trim of a door casing without mitering. A popular find at architectural salvage warehouses, rosettes are relatively inexpensive and perfect for adaptive reuse.

INSTRUCTIONS

1 Before buying the clock movement, measure the rosette's width to determine the size of the shaft you will need. Clock movements come with shafts of various lengths to fit clocks of different widths, so it's best to know how thick your clock is before purchasing your clock movement.

2 Clamp the rosette to the work surface, and with the tape measure or ruler, find the center of the piece. Mark it with the pencil.

3 With the awl or nail, press a dimple where you made your pencil mark. This will help prevent the drill bit from slipping.

4 To minimize chipping, place a piece of masking tape on the front of the rosette where the hole is to be drilled.

5 Drill a pilot hole into the center of the rosette.

6 To prevent the rosette from splitting, redrill the hole with increasingly larger bits until you have a hole just big enough for the clock movement shaft.

7 Measure and cut the molding for the brace on the back of the rosette.

8 Lay the rosette on its face, and glue the molding in place.

9 Use the spring clamps to keep the molding in place while the glue dries.

10 Once the glue is dry, insert the shaft of the clock movement from the back of the clock through your drilled hole, and up into the clock face.

11 Attach the hands according to the clock movement's instructions.

Timekeeping systems are available in inexpensive, ready-to-go kits. Any craft store will sell you a single, small package that contains everything you need to make your clock run.

DESIGNER
PAULA HEYES

MATERIALS

Rosette block

Masking tape

*Cove molding
(or any convenient piece that will help the clock stand upright)*

Wood glue

Quartz, battery-operated clock movement with hands

TOOLS

Tape measure or ruler

2 spring clamps

Pencil

Awl (or nail)

Drill with assorted bits

Handsaw

"I don't like taking complete credit for this project. My son and I were browsing through an architectural salvage warehouse, throwing out ideas to each other, when he almost tripped over a box of rosettes. 'Hey, one of these would make a good clock,' he said. And so it did."

—*Paula Heyes*

CABINET DOOR PICTURE FRAME

Frame your cherished artwork in an old and nearly forgotten cabinet door. Depending on the weight of the door you are using, you may wish to hang the frame from the cabinet door's original hinges. Or, the hinges can simply be used as an embellishment.

INSTRUCTIONS

1. Carefully pry the molding off the paneled area of the cabinet with the cat's paw.

2. Glue the removed molding together.

3. With the paint scraper, clear the panel of any chipped paint or dirt so the area will be smooth.

4. Measure the paneled area, and have a piece of glass cut to fit over the panel. For detailed instructions on cutting glass, see page 22.

5. Place the artwork along with the frame package in place over the panel.

6. Place the glass over the print.

7. Nail the molding back in place with the brads. Make sure to angle the brads so they enter the cabinet wood and don't hit the glass.

8. To hang the door by its hinges, make sure to either hang it from a stud or use the appropriate anchors to support the weight of the door. Otherwise, use standard picture-hanging hardware.

The instructions for this project will vary depending on the door you find. If you can't find a door with molding around the panel, cut your own decorative molding to place inside the panel.

DESIGNER
ROLF HOLMQUIST

MATERIALS

Cabinet door, with original hinges, if possible

Wood glue

Glass, cut to fit paneled area of door

Artwork of your choice

Frame package

Brads

Screws, to hang door from its hinges (optional)

Picture-hanging hardware

Anchors

TOOLS

Cat's paw (pry bar)

Paint scraper

Tape measure or ruler

Glass cutter (optional)

Hammer

MESSAGE WINDOW MOM'S

Create a kitchen command center with this creative project the whole family will enjoy making and using. Test out different shapes and sizes of windows until you come up with the perfect match for your family's needs.

INSTRUCTIONS

1
Remove the glass from the window frame (see page 23 for instructions on removing glass from window frames).

2
Measure the inside dimensions of each pane in your window. Be sure you are measuring from the back side.

3
Measure, mark, and cut the fiberboard or plywood to fill all the panes in your window frame.

4
Paint one (or more) of your boards with blackboard paint.

5
Roll out a small amount of cork sheeting. Place a board on top of the sheeting, and use the board as a template to cut out the cork with a craft knife.

6
Use hot glue (or adhesive of your choice) to adhere the cork to your board(s).

7
Place your covered and painted boards in the window frame. Secure them with the staples or small nails.

8
Attach the two screw eyes to the back of the frame.

9
Measure a length of picture wire to stretch between the two eyes.

10
Add 3 inches (7.6 cm) to the length of the wire, cut it, and stretch it between the two eyes. Wrap the ends of the wire back onto itself to secure the wire.

The number of panes in your window frame will determine the look of the project and dictate the amount of board and cork sheeting you will need.

DESIGNER
TERRY TAYLOR

MATERIALS

Window frame

¼ inch (6 mm) medium-density fiberboard or plywood

Blackboard paint*

Cork sheeting**

Nails or staples

2 screw eyes

Picture wire

TOOLS

Tape measure or ruler

Pencil

Handsaw

Paintbrush

Craft knife

Hot glue gun and glue sticks

*available in both spray and liquid form at home improvement stores
**available at craft stores

IRON RAIL FLOWERPOT STATION

*R*udimentary knowledge of welding and some distinctive salvaged iron are all you need to create this decorative flowerpot holder, or one similar to it.

INSTRUCTIONS

1 Measure and mark the desired location of the pot rings.

2 Use the grinder to clear any rust and paint from the welding spots.

3 Bend and cut the metal rods until the pots will hang from them without falling through.

4 Weld the rings to the iron at the desired locations.

5 Weld the brackets to the back of the iron if desired.

DESIGNER
ALAN RUARK

MATERIALS

Iron gate, rail, or pole

Metal rods

Small flowerpots

"L" brackets (optional)

TOOLS

Tape measure

Chalk

Angle grinder

Hacksaw or bandsaw

Mig welder

HOT AND COLD TOWEL RACK

This is a different take on what has become almost a convention of salvage adaptive reuse: the doorknob coatrack. Using a piece of found door molding and some salvaged faucet knobs, designer Paula Heyes created the perfect bathroom accessory.

INSTRUCTIONS

1 To create screw threads for the knobs, clamp one knob to your working surface. Place the tap, thread side down, into the knob hole. Use the tap wrench to turn the tap, creating the threads. Repeat for each knob. See page 21 for more instructions on tapping.

2 Find hex head bolts that will fit into the knob holes.

3 Measure the length of the molding to determine the placement of the knobs. Placement is based on personal preference and the length of your molding.

4 Mark the placement on the back of the molding.

5 Using the 1-inch (2.5 cm) spade bit, drill the recess for the bolt just deep enough to accommodate the head of the bolt and the washer.

6 To minimize chipping, tape the front of the molding where the hole for the knobs will be drilled.

7 Drill a pilot hole in the center of each recess.

8 Redrill with increasingly larger drill bits until the bolt fits through the hole.

9 From the back, place a washer in the recessed hole, and push the bolt through to the front. Screw on one knob. Repeat for each hole.

10 On the back, determine the placement of the hangers, and chisel out a small recess for them. Attach the hangers with the wood screws provided with them.

MATERIALS

3 porcelain hot and/or cold sink faucet knobs

Decorative door molding (as is, or cut to size)

3 hex head bolts, size depends on the size of the knob holes

3 washers

2 flat ring wall hangers

TOOLS

2 spring clamps

Tap, coarse thread*

Tap wrench

Tape measure

Masking tape

Drill with assorted bits, including a 1-inch (2.5 cm) spade bit

Chisel

Screwdriver

---

* used to create screw threads in the faucet knobs

DECORATIVE BRACKET SHELF

*D*esigner Dana Irwin
bought this bracket for a
song at an architectural
salvage warehouse, and
created this simple shelf
for her bedroom.

INSTRUCTIONS

1 Find a stud in the wall where you wish to secure your shelf.

2 Near the bottom (narrow) part of the bracket, drill a countersink hole just wide enough and deep enough to hide a screw head.

3 Drill a pilot hole for the screw, then drive the screw through the countersink hole into the bracket and wall.

4 Glue a wood plug into the countersink hole, if desired.

5 The second screw will be toenailed from the top of the bracket. Make sure you have a screw long enough to go through the bracket and into the stud at the angle you have chosen.

6 Create a countersink hole just wide enough and deep enough to hide the screw head.

7 Drill a pilot hole for the screw.

8 Make sure the bracket is level, then drive the screw through the countersink hole into the bracket and wall. Make sure the screw head is completely hidden inside the countersink hole.

9 Center and secure the glass to the bracket using the epoxy adhesive.

DESIGNER
DANA IRWIN

MATERIALS

Decorative bracket

2 wood screws

1 wood plug (optional)

Wood glue (optional)

Glass, cut to desired shape and size*

Clear epoxy adhesive

TOOLS

Stud finder (optional)

Drill with assorted bits, including a countersink bit

Screwdriver

Level

Glass cutter (optional)

---

* You can cut the glass yourself (see instructions on page 22), or if you're not sure what size and shape would look best, take the bracket to a glass retailer, and they can give you some good insights as to what will and won't work.

WINDOW BOX & TRELLIS PLANTERS

*N*ow you can enjoy the picture perfect window planter anywhere—inside or out. Or, plant your favorite creeping climbers in a pane-less variation with legs.

"In Hawaii, where I was born and raised, resources were limited because the cost of shipping was so expensive. I guess I just developed an eye for the different uses of things. When my husband and I started remodeling houses, I realized that most everything in the home could be recycled. I enjoy being able to be creative, while at the same time saving items from going into landfills."

—*Candis Killam*

DESIGNER
CANDIS L. KILLAM

MATERIALS

FOR BOX AND PLANTER

Old window frame (with or without glass)

Old wood, such as barn wood

Finish nails

Wood screws

2 heavy-duty hooks

Exterior grade polyurethane varnish

TOOLS

Tape measure

Handsaw

2 bar clamps

Try square

Hammer

Drill with 1-inch (2.5 cm) bit

Paintbrush

1 Measure the window frame to determine the length of the window box material.

2 Determine the height and width of your box before you begin.

3 Cut two boards the length of the window.

4 Cut two boards approximately 8 inches (20.3 cm) in length for the ends (though this depends on the box width you decide on).

5 Butt each end of the four boards to make a box.

6 Clamp the box together, and check the box's squareness with the try square.

7 Assemble the box with nails hammered into the front, back, and sides.

8 Measure the inside opening, and cut a bottom board to fit in the opening.

9 Drill four holes in the bottom board for drainage, using the 1-inch (2.5 cm) bit.

10 Attach the bottom of the box with nails.

11 Remove the clamps, and attach the box to the bottom of the window frame with screws. Drive screws in at 2-inch (5 cm) intervals along the bottom of the window frame.

12 Attach the two hooks on the back side of the window at the top corners.

13 Apply several coats of an exterior grade polyurethane varnish to the inside of the box (you can also paint the outside if you wish).

If you will be hanging the window box indoors, be careful of overwatering. You don't want your planter leaking onto your floor. One solution is to keep potted plants in the box.

TRELLIS PLANTER INSTRUCTIONS

Additional Materials and Tools :

Plastic garbage bag

Wood putty (optional)

Pliers

Putty knife

1 Place the window in a plastic garbage bag, and break the glass with the hammer.

2 Remove any remaining shards of glass from the frame with the pliers.

3 With the putty knife, scrape any remaining caulking from the window.

4 If the joints of the frame seem loose, fill them in with wood putty on the back side.

5 Follow the Window Box instructions on page 46 up to step number 10.

6 Cut four legs from the barn wood. Make sure each leg is the same size.

7 Attach the legs to the four corners of the planter box.

8 With the wood screws, attach barn wood scraps that are the same width as the legs to the top back portion of the planter box.

9 Attach the window to the two rear legs and the scrap wood, driving in screws at 2-inch (5 cm) intervals.

10 Apply several coats of an exterior grade polyurethane varnish to the inside of the box (you can also paint the outside if you wish).

You can use potted vines in the box, or you can place your trellis near your garden vines and train them to grow up the legs to the window frame. You can then plant complementary flowering plants in the box.

The Old, the Battered, THE CRUSTY, AND THE RUSTY

In hunting societies of the past, hunters wasted nothing of their kill. Deconstructing a home or building uses the same premise—don't throw away what can be reused. Though it would be nearly impossible to list everything that can be reclaimed from an old structure, it is certainly fun trying.

What is salvaged?

Cornices, columns, light fixtures, fireplace mantels, tile, doors, garden statuary, bathtubs, roofing slate, sinks, antique glass, beams, balustrades, paneling, radiator covers, iron fencing, molding, built-in cabinetry, light fixtures, brass hardware, windows, shutters, stair parts, posts, radiators, bricks, toilets, stoves, faucets, hardwood flooring, glass blocks, corrugated roofing tin, pressed tin, downspouts, gutters, screen doors, roof ventilators, chimney caps, piping, nails, corbels, brackets, doorknobs, hinges, window guards, building facades, gargoyles, heat registers, and iron star beam ties. What else? Anything removable and reusable.

SHUTTER PLANT STAND

Designers Molly Sieburg and Josh Malpas teamed up to create this rustic planter made from old shutters. If you don't want your plant recessed into the box, simply place a piece of marble, wood, or glass on top of the frame, and place your plant there.

**MOLLY SIEBURG &
JOSH MALPAS**

MATERIALS

4 shutters

Wood glue

Finish nails

Old lumber (for frame)

¾-inch (1.9 cm) plywood or marble, glass, etc.

4 wood screws or dowels (optional)

TOOLS

Handsaw

Circular saw or compound miter saw

Rope

Try square

Hammer

Screwdriver

Tape measure

Drill with assorted bits

1. Locate four shutters that are the same length and width. Cut to size if necessary.

2. Turn your shingles so the shutters all point in the same direction.

3. With the circular saw or miter saw, miter 45° angles on each of the edges.

4. Form a box, and glue the edges with the wood glue.

5. Tie the box tightly with the rope at the top, middle, and bottom of the box. Use the try square to check the angles.

6. When the glue is dry, further secure the frame with the nails. Remove the rope.

7. With the old lumber, fashion a frame to fit as a lip over the shutter box (see page 104 for detailed instructions on making a frame).

8. Glue the frame to the box. When the glue dries, secure further with the nails.

9. Cut a piece of plywood, glass, or marble to fit on top of the stand.

10

If you want your plant to be recessed into the stand, cut the plywood so that it just fits inside the shutter box.

11

Drill holes in the plywood for drainage.

12

Decide how far down into the box you want your plant to rest and mark the location.

13

Measure how far from the top that location is, and mark the location in all four inside corners of the box.

14

Screw the wood screws in halfway where marked, or drill holes for the dowels (see detail photo). Note: If your stand isn't wide enough to screw in the screws or drill the holes, decide on the location of the plywood plank before step 4 of the instructions.

BLUEBIRD HOUSE

The beauty of this house is that it utilizes salvaged materials in a way that is both rustic and elegant. Yours will be uniquely beautiful, too.

MATERIALS

Wood glue

Wood screws

Nails

Victorian-style ornamental molding

Dowel or peg

Wooden curtain rod end

2 inside corner moldings, 1 x 3½ (2.5 x 8.9 cm)

Old roofing shingles

Column

TOOLS

Tape measure

Pencil

Circular saw

Miter box and backsaw (optional)

2 bar clamps

Screwdriver

Hammer

Drill with assorted bits, including a 1½-inch (3.8 cm) bit

1 Cut the tongue-and-groove board into eight pieces of various lengths (the lengths of the boards range from 14 to 16 inches [35.6 to 40.6 cm]).

2 Glue the tongue-and-groove wood together in pairs, deciding at this time which pair will serve as the front.

3 With the circular saw, cut the front (A) and back (A) pieces down to 5½ inches (14 cm) wide (see figure 2 on page 53).

4 Cut the two sides (A) down to 6½ inches (16.5 cm) wide (similar to figure 2).

5 With the circular saw or miter box and backsaw, cut the tops of the front and back to a 45° angle to form a point.

6 Cut the top edge of the sides to a 45° angle to support the roof (see figure 3 on page 53).

7 With the glue, attach the runners (B) to the inside of the front, 4 inches (10.2 cm) and 7 inches (17.8 cm) from the bottom edge (this helps the young birds climb out of the house).

8 Create a box with the front, back, and side pieces. Glue them together, with the front and back pieces recessed approximately ¼ inch (6 mm) from the side edges. Clamp the box until the glue is dry.

WOOD LIST

10 to 11 linear feet (300 to 330 cm) of ¾ x 3½-inch (1.9 x 8.9 cm) tongue-and-groove wood flooring, or barn wood for house

10 inches (25.4 cm) of ¾ x 1-inch (1.9 x 2.5 cm) stock for runners

14¾ inches (37.5 cm) of ¾ x 8½-inch (1.9 x 21.6 cm) stock for roof

¾-inch (1.9 cm) board for bottom of house, measured after walls are assembled

Wood block for entrance, ¾ x 3½ x 3½ inches (1.9 x 8.9 x 8.9 cm)

Wood block for post, 3½ x 2½ x 5½ inches (8.9 x 6.4 x 14 cm)

Wood block for platform, ¾ x 4 x 4 inches (1.9 x 10.2 x 10.2 cm)

9
Reinforce the box with the screws.

10
Using the ¾-inch (1.9 cm) stock, measure for the bottom (C) of the birdhouse, and cut to fit. Recess slightly and attach with the screws.

11
Glue the roof pieces to the house, with the longer piece (D) butted with the smaller piece (E).

12
After the glue dries, reinforce with the nails.

13
Screw the entrance block (F) 6 inches (15.2 cm) up from the bottom of the house.

14
Drill a 1½-inch hole (3.8 cm) through the center of the entrance and the front of the house.

15
Glue the molding (G) under the eaves.

16
Drill a hole through the front, into the bottom for the dowel or peg (H).

17
Glue the curtain rod end (I) to the center of the roof.

18
Glue the two pieces of molding (J) to the rooftop, on either side of the curtain rod end.

CUTTING LIST

Code	Description	Qty.	Material	Dimensions
A	Tongue and groove walls	8	¾ x 3½" (1.9 x 8.9 cm)	14 to 16" (35.6 to 40.6 cm) long
B	Runners	2	¾ x 1" (1.9 x 2.5 cm)	5" (12.7 cm) long
C	Floor	1	¾" (1.9 cm) stock	*
D	Roof 1	1	¾ x 8½" (1.9 x 21.6 cm)	7¾" (19.7 cm) long
E	Roof 2	1	¾ x 8½" (1.9 x 21.6 cm)	7" (17.8 cm) long
F	Entrance	1	¾ x 3½" (1.9 x 8.9 cm)	3½" (8.9 cm) long
L	Post	1	3½ x 2½" (8.9 x 6.4 cm)	5½" (14 cm) long
M	Platform	1	¾ x 4" (1.9 x 10.2 cm)	4" (10.2 cm) long

* Length determined after the house is assembled

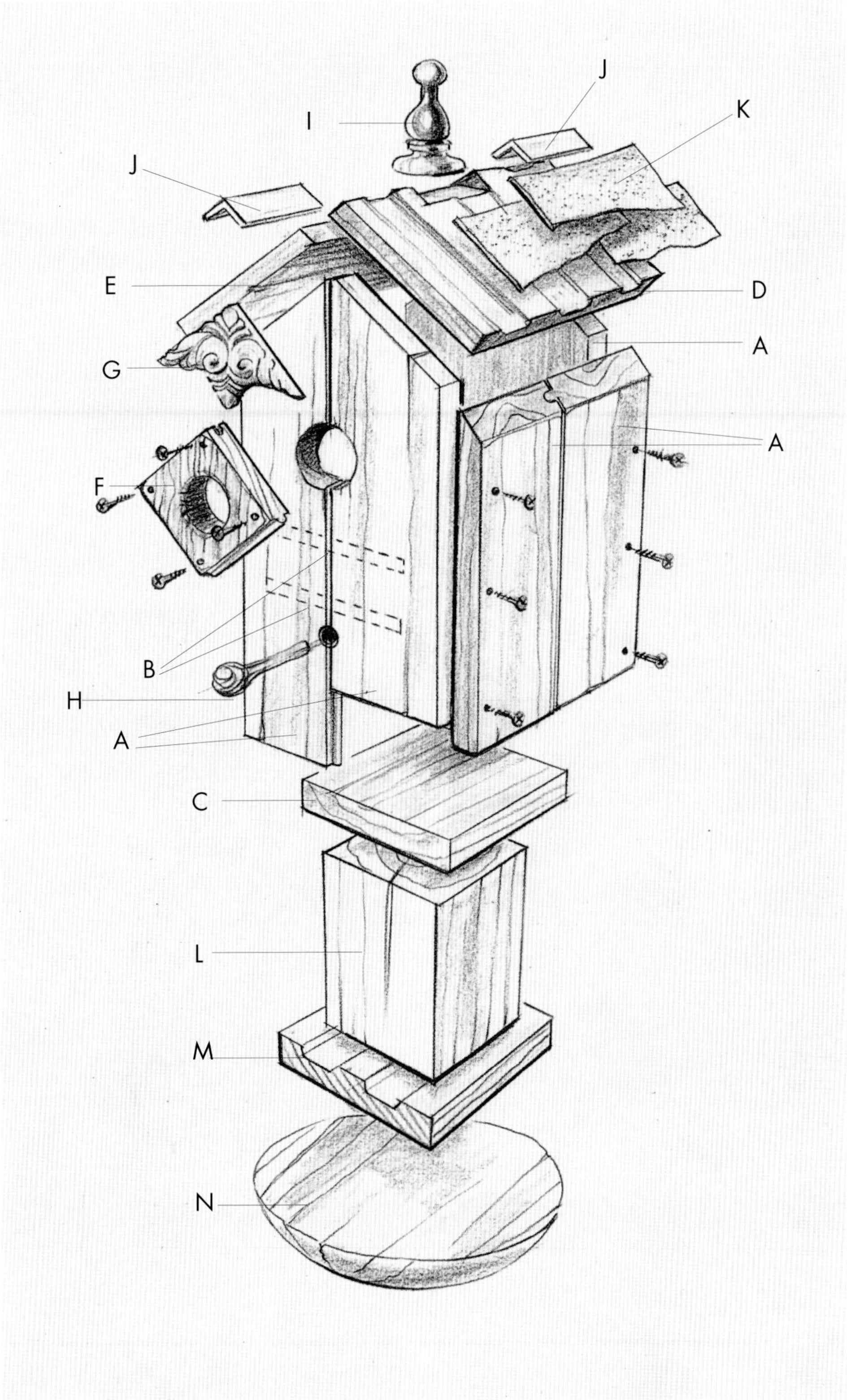

19

Nail the shingles (K) to the roof.

20

Glue the post block (L) to the bottom of the house.

21

Nail the platform (M) to the block.

22

Attach the birdhouse to the column's capital (N).

The best height for attracting bluebirds is between 5 and 10 feet (1.5 and 3 m).

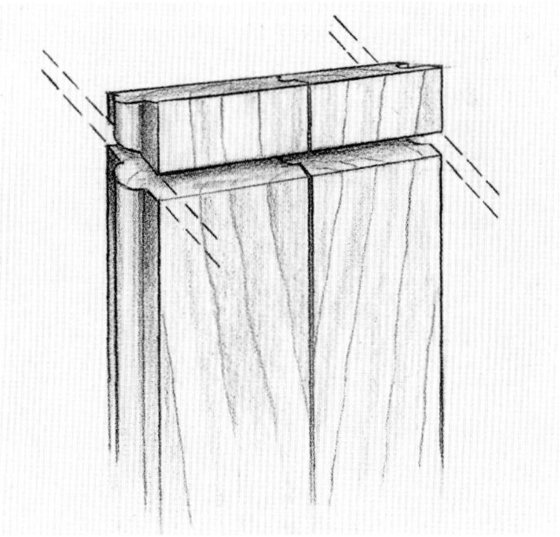

Figure 2

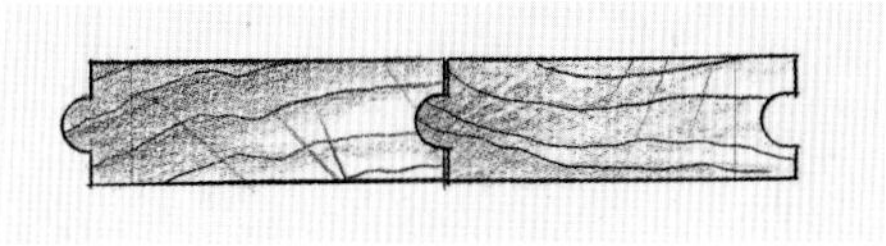

Figure 3

RUSTIC AND REFINED SHELF

*T*his study in contrasts combines weathered barn wood with decorative pressed tin ceiling panel, creating a simple, yet intriguing, stand-alone shelf.

DESIGNER
JESSE LEE

MATERIALS

Decorative pressed tin panel

Barn wood, or other weathered wood*

Tin nails

Finish nails

TOOLS

Hammer

Block of scrap wood

Tin snips

Tape measure

Handsaw

2 bar clamps

Level

Try square

---

*The wood for this particular shelf measures ½ x 5½ inches (1.3 x 14 cm).

INSTRUCTIONS

1. If the tin has uneven edges, place the tin on a hard, flat surface and hammer the edges using the block of wood as a buffer between the hammer and the tin.

2. Cut the edges of the tin (if necessary) until its length and width are consistent throughout.

3. For the sides of the stand, cut two pieces of the wood 2 to 3 inches (5 to 8 cm) longer than the length of the tin.

4. Cut the shelves the width of the tin.

5. Form a box with 2- to 3-inch (5 to 8 cm) legs using two of the shelves and the sides.

6. Clamp the box from the sides.

7. Make sure the shelves are level.

8. Use the try square to ensure that the shelf is square.

9. Place the box facedown, and place the tin over it, with the decorative side facing down.

10. Make sure the shelves and sides line up with the edges of the tin, and attach the tin to the box with the tin nails. Hammer the nails in at about 1-inch (2.5 cm) intervals around the entire border of the box.

11. Position the final shelf, make sure it is level, and nail it to the sides of the shelf.

"A farmer gave me about 5,000 tobacco sticks (used to dry tobacco), and that started me on my career of using recycled wood. I fell in love with the creative process. And I like learning to work with other people's junk and scraps. I get a true sense of enjoyment from recycling anything I know is just going to rust or rot away."

—*Jesse Lee*

IRON CORNER SHELF

...*B*righten up a bare corner with (of all things) an old porch support column. Add some glass shelves and it becomes an unusual and ornate shelf for vases, dolls, knickknacks, and more.

1 Decide whether or not the column needs any cleaning or brushing.

2 Stand the column up and decide where to position the shelves. They should rest on the ornamental elements within the column.

3 Check to make sure the area where the shelves will sit is level.

4 If the area where a shelf will sit is not level, manually bend the iron pieces until corrected.

5 Have the glass cut to fit each area where the shelves will go. I took the column to a glass cutter, and together we discussed what dimensions the shelves should be.

6 Place the glass in each area to test the fit. Two sides of the glass should be resting on ornamental iron pieces on both sides of the column, leaving the back of the glass with no support.

7 Make sure the glass is level, and mark on the column with the grease pencil where the glass needs support.

8 Drill a pilot hole for the sheet metal screws in the back of the support where marked.

9 Screw in the sheet metal screws three-quarters of the way into the drilled holes.

10 Test to make sure the shelf is still level.

11 Use the clear silicone adhesive to glue the shelves to their locations.

For maximum stability, use the holes that appear at the base of the column to screw the column to the floor. If that is not an option, create a base for the column with a wide piece of plywood painted to match the color of the column. Or, build a more elaborate base like the one created for the Baluster Candleholder on page 70.

MATERIALS

Iron porch support column

Glass, cut to fit

Sheet metal screws

Clear silicone adhesive

TOOLS

Wire brush (optional)

Level

Grease pencil

Drill with assorted bits

Screwdriver

BALUSTER LAMP

This cleverly designed lamp lends a stately presence to a dining room, bedroom, or wherever you'd like to make a creative statement.

INSTRUCTIONS

1 Prepare the base as desired.

2 Mark the center point of the base, and drill a ¼-inch (6 mm) pilot hole in the center.

3 Drill a second ¼-inch (6 mm) pilot hole in the side of the base for the wire to pass through.

4 Drill a 1⅛-inch (3 cm) center hole three-quarters of the way through the back of the base.

5 Drill a 7⁄16-inch (1.1 cm) hole through the board on the top side. Sand well.

6 Trim the bottoms of the balusters until level.

7 Choose the baluster that will be in the center of the lamp, and drill a 7⁄16-inch (1.1 cm) hole all the way through its center. You need to use a drill bit that is long enough to drill halfway through the piece you're drilling.

8 Turn the baluster over and continue drilling until you have drilled through the piece.

9 Attach the side balusters to the base by countersinking the two screws through the bottom of the base and into the columns.

10 Insert the threaded rod that comes with the lamp kit through the bottom of the base. Place the center column over the rod.

11 Wire the lamp, following the instructions that come with the kit.

12 Glue the felt to the bottom of the base.

13 Screw in the bulb, and attach the harp, shade, and finial.

*Sold in home improvement centers; lamp parts include ⅜-inch (1 cm) threaded rod, 1-inch (2.5 cm) washer with matching check rings, lock washers, nipple, nuts, hex nuts, relacquered brass pipe, socket base, push-socket, cross bar, 16- or 18-gauge stranded lamp wire, and plug.
**Tools needed for step 11.

DESIGNER
DANA IRWIN

MATERIALS

Piece of wood for base

3 short balusters

2 wood screws

Bottle lamp kit*

White craft glue

Felt

Light bulb

Lamp harp

Lamp shade

Finial

TOOLS

Tape measure

Pencil

Drill with assorted bits

Saw

Sandpaper

Screwdriver

Pipe cutter**

Hacksaw**

File**

Pliers**

Needle-nose pliers**

Sharp knife**

Glue

IVO'S CHRISTMAS TREE

DESIGNERS
**IVO BALLENTINE &
ROBIN CAPE**

*T*his project is a fun alternative to a real or artificial holiday tree. Ivo's tree looks good painted and decorated or just left alone. Hang lights, string popcorn, or wrap the tree with a thin wire and hang decorations.

MATERIALS

2 to 4 old doors*

4 to 8 hinges

Wood screws

TOOLS

*Long straightedge ruler or
long, straight board*

Pencil

Circular saw

Screwdriver

Rubber hammer

** For best results, use 5- or
6-panel doors.*

"**Try to find doors that are beyond repair. They make a more natural-looking tree, plus old 5- and 6-panel doors in good condition are quite expensive.**"

*— Ivo
Ballentine*

INSTRUCTIONS

1
Lay the first door on a flat surface, and lay the straightedge or board diagonally across it.

2
With the pencil, draw a straight line from one diagonal to the next.

3
Cut the door with the circular saw.

4
Turn the "upside-down" portion over so you have two triangles with their pointed sides up.

5
Attach the two pieces with two hinges.

6
Stand the "tree half" up, and use the rubber hammer to push the panels out a little bit. Stagger the panels to create a more treelike appearance.

7
Repeat these instructions with a second door for a complete tree (though using four doors would make the tree look fuller).

WINDOW WINDOW ON THE WALL...

For the fairest window frame mirror of all, don't settle for a run-of-the-mill rectangular window. A little salvage yard shopping will most probably yield a distinctive frame that will practically scream at you, "Take me home!"

INSTRUCTIONS

1 With the window facedown, trace the patterns of each of the panes on the tracing paper.

2 To remove the glass without breaking it, use a flat-head screwdriver or chisel to remove the old glaze or caulk. Pick out the glass from the frame. If the glass is not needed, place the window in the plastic garbage bag, and break the glass with the hammer. Remove any remaining shards of glass from the frame with the pliers. With the screwdriver or chisel, scrape off any remaining caulking.

3 With the pliers, remove any brads or staples embedded in the wood frame.

4 If the joints of the frame seem loose, fill them in with wood putty on the backside.

5 Place the traced templates over the mirror, and cut out the pane shapes with the glass cutter. For more information on glass cutting, see page 22.

6 Position each mirror piece into its pane, and secure with the glass brads.

7 Silicone the panes around the edges on the non-mirrored side.

8 Attach the picture hooks if the window will hang from a wall.

"I find my windows at junkyards, salvage yards, old houses being demolished, antique and junk stores, and auctions. If the window I'm going to be using is covered with too many layers of paint, I leave it outside and let the weather take care of it for awhile. Then I use a wire brush and some sandpaper to remove loose paint and dirt. Finally, for the really tough cases, I'll use furniture stripper or paint remover. Sometimes I'll use a color wash, stain, paint, or a collage even. I like adding coat hooks, shelves, floral patterns, and found sculpture to my mirrors. And then there are times I leave the window frame just like it is."

—*Suzanne Gustafson*

You can buy mirror in any size at glass and mirror retailers. For the best results, buy ⅛- to ¼-inch-thick (3 mm to 6 mm) mirror. And of course, if cutting mirror is beyond your scope of interest, simply take your frame or templates to a glass retailer, and they will do it for a nominal fee.

DESIGNERS

SUZANNE GUSTAFSON & PATTI HORTON-BLACKNIGHT

MATERIALS

Window

Tracing paper

Wood putty (optional)

Mirror

Glass brads

Clear silicone caulking

Heavy-duty picture hooks (optional)

TOOLS

Pencil

Flat-head screwdriver or chisel

Large plastic garbage bag (optional)

Hammer

Pliers

Putty knife

Glass cutter

Caulking gun

GARDEN FLAGS

Tired of those splashy summer watermelon flags and winter snowflake banners your neighbors put out? Then distinguish yourself with these decorative, yet simple (definitely not splashy) flags made from salvaged tin roof shingles.

1 Using the straightedge and pencil, draw a straight line diagonally from one corner of the shingle to the other.

2 Cut along the line with the tin snips to create two flags.

3 Draw designs (hearts, stars, etc.) on the cardboard.

4 Cut out the designs with the scissors to create templates.

5 Trace the templates onto the tin.

6 Drill a small hole inside each of the traced outline shapes.

7 Use the tin snips to cut out the shapes.

8 Drill three screw holes along the edge of each flag.

9 Paint the flags with the brass or copper paint, if so desired.

10 Attach the finial to the top of the pole with the adhesive bond.

11 Screw the flags to the pole.

MATERIALS

14 x 18-inch (35.6 x 45.7 cm) piece of galvanized tin roof shingle

Cardboard

Brass or copper paint (optional)

Drapery end finial

Adhesive bond

6 wood screws

Pole

TOOLS

Straightedge ruler

Pencil

Tin snips

Scissors

Drill with assorted bits

Screwdriver

RECYCLED BAR

*G*uests will be

sure to rave about

this sturdy, versatile

bench no matter

where you put it or

how you use it.

Replace your

microwave cart in

the kitchen, serve

drinks in the dining

room or out in the

backyard, or pot

your plants in style.

DESIGNER

BILL ALEXANDER

MATERIALS

Assorted salvaged lumber,
1 x 8

Assorted salvaged lumber,
1 x 10

Window, no more than 30 inches
(76.2 cm) wide or tall

Finish nails

TOOLS

Tape measure

Handsaw

Hammer

Framing square

INSTRUCTIONS

1 Measure and record the width and height of the window to be used for this project.

2 Cut two side pieces from the 1 x 8 boards to match the height of the window (A). See the illustration on page 68.

3 Nail the side pieces to the window, flush with the rear of the window (A).

4 Cut the top and bottom pieces from the 1 x 10 boards 2 inches (5 cm) longer than the width of the window (B).

5 Nail the top and bottom pieces (B) to the window, and set aside.

6 For the base sides, cut six 1 x 10 boards 35 inches (88.9 cm) long (C), or you can use six 1 x 8 boards.

7 Lay the six boards on the ground in two sets of three with the inside facing up. Use the framing square to make sure they are lined up and level.

8 Rip two 1 x 8 boards in half.

9 Cut the four resulting 1 x 4s so they are 2 inches (5 cm) shorter than the combined width of the base sides (28 inches [71.1 cm] if using 1 x 10 boards). These will be the crosspieces that attach the base sides (D).

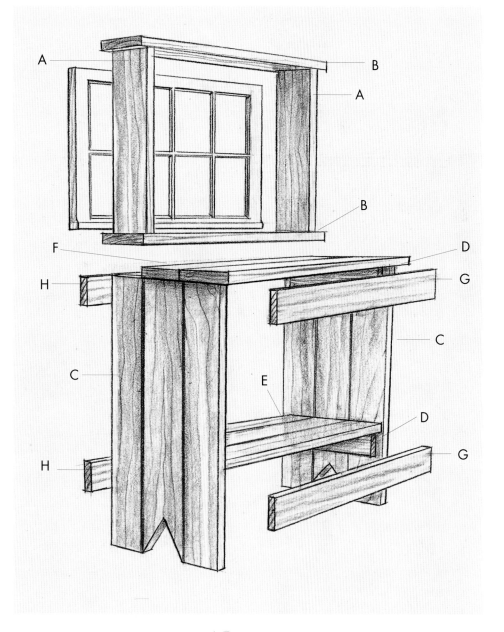

14

Nail the boards to the top of the lower crosspieces (E). The back edge of the shelf should be flush with the back ends of the crosspieces, while the front edge should extend out no more than 1 inch (2.5 cm).

15

Attach the window unit to the completed base by nailing the bottom board to the top of each base side, leaving a 1-inch (2.5 cm) overhang on each side. The back side of the window should be flush with the back edges of the base sides.

16

Cut the two 1 x 10 boards needed for the top of the base to the length of the bottom board attached to the window (F). Nail the boards to the top of the base with a 1-inch (2.5 cm) overhang in front.

17

Rip a 1 x 8 board in half.

18

Cut the two resulting 1 x 4 boards to the width of the base (G).

19

Nail the 1 x 4 boards to the ends of the crosspieces that show in front (G).

20

Nail two 1 x 8 boards to the ends of the crosspieces that show in back (H).

Remove the glass from the window, and use the frame to drape towels, gardening gloves, or napkins.

10

Nail the top crosspieces (D) flush with the top of the base sides. Leave a 1-inch (2.5 cm) space between both ends of the crosspieces and sides.

11

Nail the bottom crosspieces (D) 6 or 7 inches (15.2 or 17.8 cm) up from the bottom of the boards. Leave a 1-inch (2.5 cm) space between both ends of the crosspieces and sides.

12

Mark and cut "V" notches out of the center boards of each base side, if desired.

13

For the bottom shelf, cut three 1 x 10 boards the width of the window (E).

The Search

S alvage hunting is not relegated simply to visiting your local salvage warehouse or yard. There are plenty of ways to find that perfect iron gate for your living room.

■ Check the buisness section of your phone book under "Salvage," "Building Materials," "Salvage and Surplus," "Antiques," "Junk," and/or "Demolition."

■ Upscale garden shops now often deal in architectural salvage for decorating gardens and yards.

■ Dumpsters at demolition sites often offer up a few gems that can only be filed under "people throw away the darnedest things."

■ Garage sales and yard sales can yield a true (usually quite cheap) find.

■ Check your local paper for estate auctions.

■ Search online directories for "Architectural Salvage."

■ Call demolition contractors. You can ask them where they take their dumpsters, or even ask them if you can look at the pieces they are finding at a demolition site.

■ Call your local historic preservation society, and ask if they have a salvage warehouse or other services. Or you can ask them if they know of any salvagers in the area.

■ Search online, though you may have to relegate your search to smaller objects. Shipping costs can be prohibitive. Use message boards and forums when looking for specific items.

■ Place classified ads in magazines that specialize in old house restoration.

■ Talk to carpenters, general contractors, metal workers, etc. Find out if they or someone they know works with recycled materials.

"Architecture is frozen music."

—FRIEDRICH WILHELM JOSEPH VON SCHELLING

DESIGNER

JEAN TOMASO MOORE

BALUSTER CANDLEHOLDER

One or more of these candleholders will literally brighten up any room. Designer Jean Moore has included detailed instructions for creating a base with decorative molding distressed to match the baluster—a wonderful touch that can be added if time or resources permit.

MATERIALS

Old baluster

2 x 6 board, for base

2-inch (5.1 cm) decorative molding, approximately 2½ feet (75 cm) per base

Brads

Acrylic craft paints to match baluster paint

Heavy-duty adhesive bond

Wood screws

Candle, 1-inch (2.5 cm) wide

TOOLS

Handsaw

Level

Straightedge ruler

Pencil

Drill with assorted bits, including a 1-inch (2.5 cm) bit

Miter box and backsaw

Hammer

Nail set

Paintbrush

Screwdriver

INSTRUCTIONS

1 Cut any uneven or broken pieces off the baluster.

2 Decide which end will accommodate the candle, and make sure the baluster is level.

3 Drill a 1-inch (2.5 cm) hole into the center of the baluster top where the candle will go. For best results, test the candle's fit by first drilling into a piece of scrap wood.

4 Decide how large you want your base to be. The base must accommodate the shape and height of the baluster—the wider the base, the more stable the candleholder (bases for these candlesticks were between 4½ [11.4 cm] and 6½ inches [16.5 cm] square).

5 Cut out the base block from the 2 x 6 board.

6 Measure and cut the molding (if decorating the base) to the size of the base.

7 Miter the corners of the molding.

8 Attach the molding to the base with the brads.

9 Use a nail set to tap the brads into the wood.

10 To distress-paint the base to match the color of the baluster, first use a watered-down brown "wash" for the first coat.

11 Allow it to dry, and then brush and rub in layers of the top color, striving to simulate the aged look of the original paint colors of the baluster.

12 To attach the baluster to the base, place the baluster on the center of the base, and draw a pencil outline around the baluster onto the base.

13 Apply a thin layer of the glue to the bottom of the baluster, and place the baluster on the center of the base.

14 After the glue dries, turn the candleholder upside down, and reinforce with a wood screw.

OLD DOOR FUTON SOFA

$\mathcal{I}$f you're up to a woodworking challenge, this beautiful full-sized futon sofa could soon grace your living room, den, spare room, or porch. The old door is a wonderful detail that will truly stand out in a contemporary setting.

GEORGE HARRISON

MATERIALS

4 to 6 panel door, cut to 29 inches (73.7 cm) in width

36 screws, 2½ inches (6.4 cm)

36 wood plugs, ⅜ inch (9.5 mm) in diameter

4 corner blocks

Wood glue

33 finishing nails, 1½ inches (3.8 cm)

2 carriage bolts, ⅜ x 3 inches (9.5 mm x 7.6 cm)

2 dowel pins, ½ inch (1.3 cm) in diameter, 3 inches (7.6 cm) long

2 dowel pins, 1 inch (2.5 cm) in diameter, 2¾ inches (7 cm) long

TOOLS

Tape measure

Circular saw or table saw

Router (optional)

2 web clamps

Drill with assorted bits, including a ⅜-inch countersink bit

Screwdriver

Handsaw and chisel (optional)

Hammer

Wrench

Nail set

INSTRUCTIONS

Side Assembly (figure 1)

1 Cut the door into 2 pieces, each 23¾ inches high (60.3 cm) and 29 inches (73.7 cm) wide (A). Make sure a door rail is centered at 10⅜ inches (26.4 cm) from the floor for each piece.

2 Cut the two armrests (B).

3 Shape the armrests, if so desired, with the router.

4 Position the armrests on top of the door pieces. Make sure that the inside edge of each armrest is flush with the inside edge of each door piece.

5 Clamp each armrest to the door panel, and drill three evenly spaced ⅜-inch countersink holes where the screws will go.

6 Attach the armrests to the door panels with three 2½-inch (6.4 cm) screws through the countersink holes.

7 Using a dab of wood glue, adhere the wood plugs over the screw heads. Follow the countersink and wood plug instructions wherever you use the screws.

8 Measure and mark 8 inches (20.3 cm) from the rear of each door panel and 11½ inches (29.2 cm) from the bottom

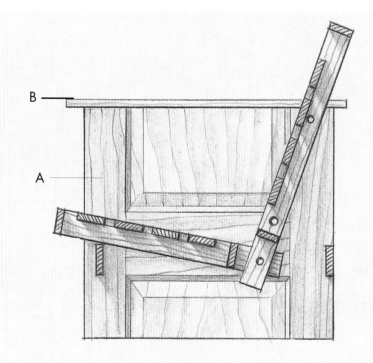

Figure 1

WOOD LIST

5½ linear feet (165 cm) of 1 x 5"
(2.5 x 12.7 cm) stock

47 linear feet (14.1 m) of 1 x 2½"
(2.5 x 6.4 cm) stock

4¼ linear feet (127.5 cm) of
1 x 1¾" (2.5 x 4.4 cm) stock

49 linear feet (15 m) of ¾ x 3½"
(1.9 x 8.9 cm) stock

CUTTING LIST

Code	Description	Qty.	Material	Dimensions
SIDES				
A	Door pieces	2		29 x 23¾" (73.7 x 60.3 cm)
B	Armrests	2	1 x 5" (2.5 x 12.7 cm)	33" (83.8 cm) long
FRAME				
C	Stretcher rails	2	1 x 2½" (2.5 x 6.4 cm)	75" (190.5 cm) long
D	Corner blocks	4		
DECK BACK				
E	Sides	2	1 x 2½" (2.5 x 6.4 cm)	32" (81.3 cm) long
F	Top	1	1 x 2½" (2.5 x 6.4 cm)	75" (190.5 cm) long
G	Bottom	1	1 x 2½" (2.5 x 6.4 cm)	73" (185.4 cm) long
H	Middle	1	1 x 1¾" (2.5 x 4.4 cm)	24½" (62.2 cm) long
I	Slats	4	4 x 3½" (1.9 x 8.9 cm)	73¹⁰⁄₁₆" (187 cm) long
DECK FRONT				
J	Sides	2	1 x 2½" (2.5 x 6.4 cm)	25½" (64.8 cm) long
K	Top	1	1 x 2½" (2.5 x 6.4 cm)	72¹⁵⁄₁₆" (185.3 cm) long
L	Bottom	1	1 x 2½" (2.5 x 6.4 cm)	70¹⁵⁄₁₆" (180.2 cm) long
M	Middle	1	1 x 1¾" (2.5 x 4.4 cm)	24½" (62.2 cm) long
N	Slats	4	¾ x 3½" (1.9 x 8.9 cm)	71½" (181.6 cm) long

of each door panel. This is where the 1-inch (2.5 cm) dowel will enter, securing the futon deck to the frame. This mark must be located at a door rail, not on a panel.

Drill a hole three-quarters of the way through the door rail from the inside, at the location just marked.

Frame Assembly

Cut the two stretcher rails (C).

Attach the stretcher rails to the sides using two screws on each side of the door panel. Each stretcher rail should be fastened 7½ inches (19.1 cm) from the ground, and ¼ inch (6 mm) from the back edge of the door piece (see figure 1 for placement).

With the wood glue, attach the four corner pieces (D) to the four corners created by the stretcher rails and the sides.

Drill a ½-inch (1.3 cm) hole in each of the door panels 1 inch (2.5 cm) from the top of the panels and 2¼ inches (5.7 cm) from the back.

Back Deck Assembly (figure 2)

Cut the sides (E), top (F), and bottom (G) of the back deck frame.

With the router (or handsaw and chisel), cut out a ½-inch (1.3 cm) wide and ¾-inch (1.9 cm) deep groove in the side pieces (E) for the tips of the slats to rest in.

Drill a ½-inch (1.3 cm) hole 10¼ inches (26 cm) from the top of the side pieces for the dowel pin.

Drill a 1-inch (2.5 cm) hole 23 inches (58.4 cm) from the top of the sides for the dowel.

Drill a ⅜-inch hole 28 inches (71.1 cm) from the top of the sides for the carriage bolt.

Butt the side pieces to the top piece, and use two screws on each side of the top piece to secure the side pieces.

Attach the bottom piece 6½ inches (16.5 cm) from the bottom with two screws for each end.

Cut the middle piece (H).

Position the middle piece in the middle of the deck frame, between the front and back pieces, making sure it is flush with the back of the frame (so the slats can rest on top of the middle piece without sticking out).

Attach the middle piece with one screw on each end.

Cut the four slat pieces (I).

Position the slats evenly into the grooves cut out for them in the side pieces, and nail them into place with two nails on each end.

Front Deck Assembly (figure 2)

Cut the sides (J), top (K), and bottom (L) of the front deck frame.

With the router (or handsaw and chisel), cut out a ½ inch-wide (1.3 cm) and ¾-inch-deep (1.9 cm) groove in the

side pieces for the tips of the slats to rest in.

Drill a ⅜-inch hole 1¾ inches (4.4 cm) from the top of the side pieces.

Butt the side pieces to the top piece and attach with two screws.

Attach the bottom piece with two screws for each end so it is flush with the ends of the side pieces.

Cut the middle piece (M).

Position the middle piece in the middle of the deck frame, between the front and back pieces, making sure it is flush with the back of the frame (so the slats can rest on top of the middle piece without sticking out).

Attach the middle piece with one screw on each end.

Cut the four slat pieces (N).

Position the slats evenly into the grooves cut out for them in the side pieces, and nail them into place with two nails for each end.

Futon Sofa Assembly

With the two decks laying on the ground, line up the ⅜-inch holes in each deck (in the side pieces) and thread the carriage bolts through from the outside of the frame (figure 2).

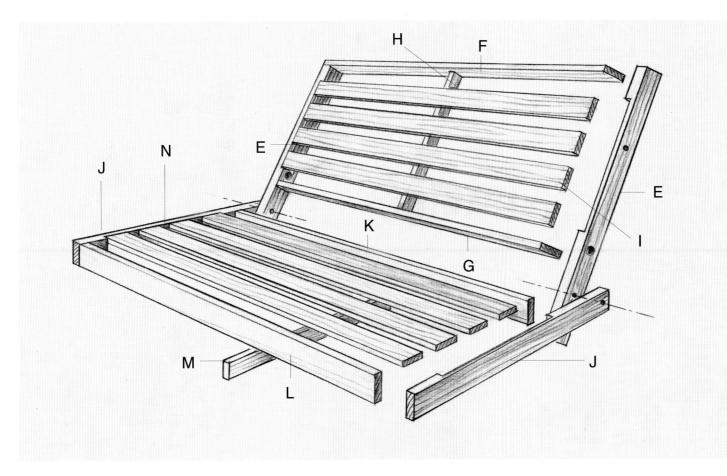

Figure 2

Tighten the bolts with nuts and washers. Make sure there is ½ inch (1.3 cm) between the deck sections (figure 3). If not, you must reconfigure the drill holes until the ½-inch (1.3 cm) space exists.

Once the bolts have been tightened, hammer the nail set into the threads outside the bolt to keep the bolt from loosening.

Place the attached decks on top of the frame, making sure the decks are in the right locations.

Raise the back deck until the dowel pin holes in the back deck and door panels align (from step 3 of the Back Deck Assembly instructions). Place the ½-inch (1.3 cm) dowel pins through the holes.

Insert the 1-inch (2.5 cm) dowels through the 1-inch (2.5 cm) holes

drilled into the back deck's side pieces in step 4 of the Back Deck Assembly instructions and into the holes drilled into the door railings in step 9 of the Side Assembly instructions.

Hammer a nail into each dowel head from the top of the side piece to keep them from falling out.

Finish the wood as desired.

BLANKET CHEST

$\mathscr{D}$esigner Ed Doyle used two old 18-inch-wide (45.7 cm) basement doors for this exquisite chest. If you want a bigger chest, simply find a bigger door. You can get away with using only one door if you don't mind what the back of the chest looks like.

MATERIALS

1 or 2 wooden doors, 5-panel pre-ferred

Wood glue

Finish nails

2 x 2 stock, for cleats

Wood screws

Salvaged boards or plywood

1 x 6 stock, for cleats

2 hinges

Old door casing (or any salvaged wood)

Wooden doorstop or small finial

TOOLS

Putty knife or paint scraper

Tape measure

Pencil

Sawbucks

Circular saw

Try square

Hammer

Screwdriver

Level

Sander

INSTRUCTIONS

1 Scrape any loose paint or finish from the door, leaving some of the cracked paint for effect.

2 Remove any hardware from the door.

3 Measure equal distances between the top panel and the bottom panel for the side cuts of the chest.

4 Lay the door faceup on the sawbucks, and set the circular saw at a 45° angle using a straightedge guide.

5 Cut the two end panels from the door.

6 Make sure the 45° cuts are in the same direction, then recut the three-panel piece to match the end pieces. The door lock mortise should be located on the bottom of the chest.

7 Fasten the three pieces together with the glue.

8 With the try square, make sure the angles are correct.

9 When the glue dries, reinforce the joints with nails.

10 Measure and cut the 2 x 2 stock to fit inside the box as cleats for the base.

11 Screw in the four cleats to the inside of the chest for the base.

12 Cut the salvaged board or plywood to fit the base, and screw it to the cleats.

13 Set the circular saw at a 45° angle using a straightedge guide, and cut the second door (or board of similar dimensions) to fit the back.

14 Nail the back piece to the sides of the frame.

15 Size the planks for the top with a ½-inch (1.3 cm) overhang all around the front and two sides and flush to the back.

Cut the planks, and glue together.

Once the glue dries, check to make sure they are level; and on the side that will face into the box, attach the 1 x 6 cleats with wood screws (this prevents cupping).

Attach the top to the chest with the hinges and screws.

Cut the old door casing to fit as the trim on the bottom to cover the door knob hole. Miter the corners of the trim 45°.

Add the doorstop or a small finial as a handle.

Shopping TIPS

There are a few things to keep in mind before going out on a salvage hunt.

- Most salvage centers do not keep a 9-to-5 business schedule. Always call first.

- Wear old clothes. Bring gloves if you know you'll to be handling old lumber.

- Bring a measuring tape.

- Bring a pen knife to check for punky wood.

- If you are looking for something specific, bring along a photo or a sketch.

- Don't be afraid to haggle, but also be prepared to pay the asking price.

- Don't look for perfect pieces. The cracks, rust, bumps, and bruises add character to the piece anyway.

- If you know where in your home a certain piece is going to go, measure the area first to make sure the piece you find will fit.

- Ask questions.

- Have an open mind, be prepared to come home with something completely unexpected, and if you fall in love with something, buy it. It may not be there next time.

"Architecture is my delight, and putting up and pulling down one of my favorite amusements."
—A STATEMENT ATTRIBUTED TO THOMAS JEFFERSON

STAND-ALONE CUPBOARD

A vintage farmhouse door has been combined with a pair of old kitchen cabinets to create a sturdy, freestanding cupboard that evokes memories of days gone by.

1 Find old cabinets that are smaller in width than the door. Find a combination that works for you and that will let the structure stand by itself without tipping over. The bottom cabinet needs to be flush with the ground when the assembly is standing up.

2 Remove the backs from the cabinets.

3 Lay the door on the ground, and position the cabinets to your satisfaction. Cut the cabinets if you need to.

4 With the jigsaw, create ¾-inch (1.9 cm) cutouts in the back of the cabinets on both sides (see detail photo below). Depending on the size of the cabinets, two cutouts may be necessary.

5 With the jigsaw, cut out rounded-off sections of the scrap wood to act as tabs that will attach to the door and the cabinets (see detail photo below).

6 Nail the rounded-off scrap wood into each cutout with the rounded-off section sticking out.

7 Cut the old board to fit as a shelf for the bottom cabinet.

8 Nail the shelf into place.

9 Place the door on the ground, and position the cabinets so that the bottom cabinet is flush with the bottom of the door.

10 Screw the cabinet tabs to the door.

MATERIALS

Old door

Salvaged kitchen cabinets, smaller in width than the door

¾-inch-thick (1.9 cm) scrap wood

Old board

Nails

Wood screws

TOOLS

Tape measure

Handsaw

Jigsaw

Hammer

Screwdriver

HEAT REGISTER BENCH

$\mathscr{D}$esigner Dana Irwin teamed up with welder Alan Ruark to create this sturdy garden bench

that perfectly highlights the lovely patterns of the salvaged heat registers.

DESIGNER

DANA IRWIN

MATERIALS

2 register grates

Primer

Paint

Steel needed:

Filler metal

1½-inch (3.8 cm) angle steel for around the outside of the grate frame

2 x 2-inch (5.1 x 5.1 cm) tubing between the grates

1 x ¼-inch (2.5 cm x 6 mm) flat stock for the grate support tabs

1½-inch (3.8 cm) square tubing for the legs

½-inch (1.3 cm) square solid stock for the horizontal braces and the triangle detail

4 small cast steel balls

TOOLS

Angle grinder

Sanding pad or wire brush (optional)

Tape measure

Chalk

Chopsaw

Bandsaw

Clamps

Framing square

Level

Mig welder

INSTRUCTIONS

1. Remove each grate from its assembly. Clean the grates with the angle grinder or with a sanding pad or wire brush.

2. Measure, mark, and cut your angle steel to the dimensions you desire, keeping in mind that you want your grates to be flush with the frame.

3. Cut the ends of the angle steel at a 45° angle for mitered joints.

4. Cut the 2 x 2 (5.1 x 5.1 cm) tubing to fit in the middle of the frame.

5. Notch the ends so you can weld it underneath the frame and it will still be flush with the top.

6. Tack your frame together, and check that your grates fit properly and that everything is square.

7. Weld the frame together. Each piece should be clamped to your work space before welding.

8. Weld small tabs just underneath the frame to support the grates.

9. Cut the 1½-inch (3.8 cm) tubing for the legs, taking into consideration the frame and any feet you may want to add when determining the height.

10. Fit the legs inside the corners of the frame, and weld them into place.

11. Use the ½-inch (1.3 cm) stock for the triangles. Weld the pieces to the hori-zontal braces and to the inside of the frame.

12. Smooth your welds with the grinder.

13. Weld the steel balls to the bottom of the legs.

14. Prime and paint your bench.

"In my basement, I have several nice cast iron pieces for projects I have designed. They're just waiting for me to take a welding class so I can finish them!"

—Dana Irwin

PORCH BALUSTER SIDE TABLE

*T*his delightful little table takes no time at all to put together, but it will provide a lifetime of charm, even in the most inconspicuous of corners.

1   Form a box with the four balusters by forming butt joints.

2   Glue the box together.

3   After the glue dries, reinforce the box with the nails.

4   Center the salvaged wood on top of the baluster boards, and nail it to the top of the balusters.

5   If you had to cut the tabletop, "weather" the cut side with brown paint.

"When I find an interesting detail, I never know what I'll make at first. I just know that if it's a good thing, something nice will come along."

—Rolf Holmquist

DESIGNER
ROLF HOLMQUIST

MATERIALS

4 baluster uprights

Wood glue

Finish nails

Square piece of salvaged barn wood or other weathered wood

Brown paint (optional)

TOOLS

2 bar clamps

Hammer

Paintbrush (optional)

CRAIG COMEAU

GLASS-TOP CABINET

*D*esigner Craig Comeau removed the panels from an old door and built this exquisite cabinet. The glass lid is the only difficult part of this project, but it is truly worth the effort.

1 After collecting the doors you will use, decide which sections of the doors will become the front and sides of the cabinet. Choose sections containing panels that would make good storage.

2 Cut the doors, creating the front and two sides.

3 Use the miter saw or circular saw to miter the edges of the door pieces to create three sides of the cabinet.

4 Use the router with a straight bit to remove the door panels from the door pieces (see figure 1 on page 90). Once the panels are removed you will have rabbets to accept the box compartments.

5 Nail the door pieces together with the rabbets facing inward.

6 Measure the paneled openings for your compartment box dimensions. The boxes should be 1/16 inch (1.6 mm) smaller than the dimensions of the paneled openings. The depth of the boxes needs to allow for the plywood backing.

7 Once the boxes' dimensions have been determined, cut the 3/4-inch (1.9 cm) plywood and/or 1 x 10 stock to create the compartment boxes.

8 Nail the boxes together. Add shelves to the boxes if desired.

MATERIALS

1 to 2 old panel doors

Finish nails

3/4-inch-thick (1.9 cm) plywood or 1 x 10 stock, for compartment boxes

2 x 2 stock, for cleats and braces

Screws

3/8-inch-thick (10 mm) plywood, sized to match back of cabinet

2 x 4 framing stock, sized to block the bottom of the cabinet

Assorted molding, for base and lid

Birch plywood, for lining the top compartment

Mahogany or other wood, for top opening trim

2 hinges

Glass, cut to fit top

TOOLS

Tape measure

Table saw

Miter saw or circular saw

Router

Hammer

Screwdriver

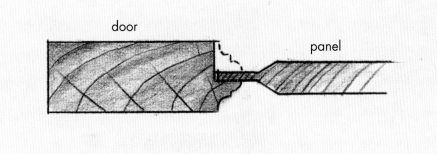

Figure 1

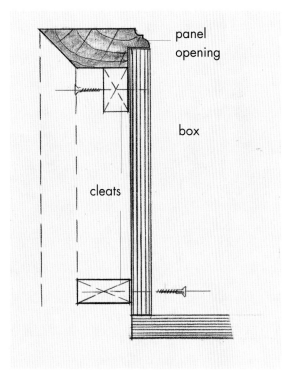

Figure 2

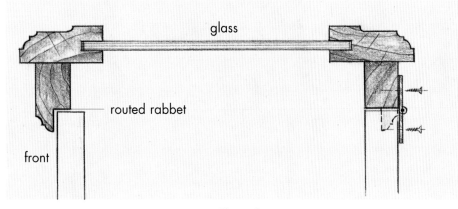

Figure 3

9 Cut out cleats for each of the boxes from the 2 x 2 stock.

10 Screw the cleats to the inside edges of the paneled openings (figure 2).

11 Screw the boxes to the cleats.

12 Measure the back opening of the cabinet, and cut four braces from the 2 x 2 stock.

13 Install the braces to the back of the cabinet, recessed in from the back of the cabinet ⅜ inch (10 mm) to accept the plywood backing.

14 Cut and nail the ⅜-inch (10 mm) plywood backing to the braces.

15 Block out the bottom of the cabinet with the 2 x 4s to provide the proper height needed for the base molding. Allow for the desired overlap of the molding over the cabinet.

16 Cut and install the base molding.

17 Measure the opening at the top of the cabinet. Cut the birch plywood to create the box in the compartment.

18 Nail the box together, and nail it into the hole.

19 Cut the mahogany or other wood to cover the top of the compartment. Nail the wood into place.

20 From the remaining old door pieces, rip 2 x 2 stock for the top frame.

21 Cut the two long pieces to fit the length of the top opening.

31 Cut to length four lid molding pieces so that they will overlap the lid frame ⅛ inch (3 mm) on all sides.

32 Dado a groove in the molding to accept the glass (figure 3).

33 Nail three pieces of the molding to the frame.

34 Measure for the glass.

35 Insert the glass and add the fourth piece of molding.

36 Carefully nail or glue the molding to the frame.

37 Replace the hinge pins to install the lid.

22 Decide which piece will serve as the front of the frame, and with the router, carve out a rabbet that will let the piece sit on the door (figure 3).

23 Measure where the rabbet begins, and mark that measurement on the rear piece.

24 Cut the rear piece at the mark (figure 3). In other words, the rear piece will not be rabbeted.

25 Position the two long pieces onto the top of the cabinet, so that the front piece overlaps the top of the cabinet and allows for a ⅛-inch (3 mm) clearance between the lid and the cabinet.

26 Measure for the side pieces that will complete the lid.

27 Rip the side pieces for the lid out of the remaining door pieces.

28 Nail the lid frame together. Check the fit before continuing.

29 Mortise two hinges onto the cabinet and lid. Install the hinges.

30 Remove the hinge pins, and separate the lid from the cabinet.

WINDOW GUARD POT RACK

Keep cookware within easy reach by hanging a salvaged window guard or iron gate from your ceiling, creating the perfect pot rack.

DESIGNER

J. DABNEY PEEPLES

MATERIALS

*Salvaged window guard
or iron gate*

Large sheet of paper

*4 large "S" hooks, plus
additional for pots and pans*

4 eye bolts

Scrap pieces of 2 x 4 stock

Nails

Heavy-duty chain

4 small "S" hooks

TOOLS

Tape measure

Pencil

Scissors

Stud finder (optional)

Drill with assorted bits

Metal clothes hanger

Handsaw

Hammer

Vise

Hacksaw

INSTRUCTIONS

Note: If you don't have an attic, you must hang the window guard from the ceiling joists, hence limiting the size and location of your rack. Measure the distance from one joist to the next, and then hunt for a salvaged window guard or iron gate that will fit.

1 Create a paper template with the same dimensions as the window guard.

2 Mark on the template where the best location would be for the large "S" hooks that will attach the chains to the window guard. Test the "S" hooks to make sure the window guard will hang from them safely.

3 Use the template to decide where you wish to hang the window guard. If there is an attic above your kitchen, you can pretty much hang it where you want.

4 Using the template, mark on the ceiling where the holes will be drilled for the eye bolts. If you don't have an attic, all four holes must be aligned with a joist. Use the stud finder to determine whether or not a joist is located above the planned holes.

5 If you don't have an attic, drill your holes once you are certain each hole will lead into a joist. Screw in the eye bolts until they are flush with the top of the ceiling.

6 If you have an attic, drill your four holes. If you've drilled into a joist, simply screw in an eye bolt until it is flush with the top of the ceiling.

7 If there is no joist for one or more of the holes, use a straightened-out metal clothes hanger and have a friend poke it through the hole. Go to the attic, and find the protruding hanger. This eliminates having to pilfer through the insulation trying to find the hole. Once you find the hole, measure the distance between the two nearest joists.

8 Cut a piece of 2 x 4 to fit snugly between the two joists (see figure 1 on page 94).

9 Make sure the 2 x 4 is directly above the hole, and nail it to the two joists (see figure 1 on page 94).

10 Screw the eye bolt through the hole in the ceiling into the secured 2 x 4 (see figure 1 on page 94).

11 Repeat for each hole in the ceiling that doesn't lead directly into a joist.

12 Once the eye bolts are fastened, decide on the length of chain needed.

Measure the chain length, and place the link just outside the desired measurement in a vise.

Cut the link with the hacksaw and discard the cut link.

Repeat until you have four chains of equal length.

Hang the chains from the eye bolts with the small "S" hooks (though you can also use eye bolts that have hooks instead of "eyes").

Connect the large "S" hooks to the bottom link of each chain.

With a friend or two, lift the window guard and hook it to the "S" hooks.

Hang additional "S" hooks on the window guard, and hang your pots and pans from them.

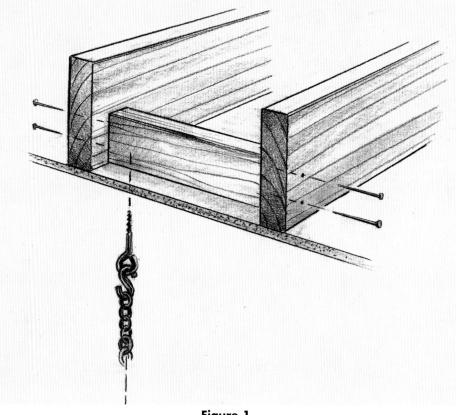

Figure 1

SALVAGED BOOKENDS

The marble lends a heft that is often missing in ornamental book-ends, while the molding adds just enough leverage and decoration.

Try using found marble just as it is to avoid having to trim it.

DESIGNER
DANA IRWIN

MATERIALS

2 salvaged marble pieces

Decorative molding

Clear silicone adhesive bond

TOOLS

5-pound hammer (optional)

Awl (optional)

Chisel (optional)

Handsaw

2 spring clamps

INSTRUCTIONS

If you're looking for a clean edge for your marble, contact a professional marble cutter.

1

If the marble you found needs some shaping, decide on where you want to cut, and score the area to be removed with the awl and hammer.

2

Use the chisel and hammer to remove the piece or pieces. This is not an exact science, so be prepared for some happy accidents. Of course, you can always take it to a marble cutter.

3

Cut the molding to fit the base of the bookends.

4

Glue the molding to the marble with the silicone adhesive bond. Wipe away any excess glue.

5

Clamp the molding to the marble for 24 hours.

OLD DOOR GARDEN DIVIDER

*H*ide the compost heap

or block an unwanted view

with several old

doors standing

up side by side.

A missing door

panel provides a

great location for

wind chimes or

a birdhouse.

DESIGNERS
ROGER LEICHTER & JOYCE YARLING

MATERIALS

Several old doors

Assorted bricks and/or stones

Several metal pipes, 6-feet (1.8 m) long

Heavy-duty plastic sheets

Several half clamps

Wood screws

TOOLS

Shovel

Sledge hammer

Scissors

Staple gun

Screwdriver

INSTRUCTIONS

1 Decide on the location of your fence or divider. Position the doors.

2 Dig holes deep enough to hold the doors upright.

3 Place assorted bricks and/or stones in the bottom of the holes (they keep the doors from standing in water).

4 Cut the plastic sheet to cover the bottom parts of the doors that will be underground.

5 Staple the plastic to the doors.

6 Position the doors in the holes, and fill in the holes with the dirt.

7 Pound the metal pipes into the ground directly behind each door. Each pipe should go 2 to 3 feet (.6 to .9 m) into the ground.

8 Fasten the poles to the doors with the half clamps and wood screws (see photo, left).

9 Decorate and landscape as desired. Cover any visible plastic with mulch.

YOU'VE GOT MAIL

*T*his is a quick and easy project. If you are lucky enough to find a shutter with an aged (and attractive) paint finish, it is a simple matter of attaching a backing to prevent those pesky bills from disappearing. If your shutter lacks an interesting paint finish, it is easy to achieve one with thinned acrylic paint and a brush.

DESIGNER
TERRY TAYLOR

MATERIALS

Shutter

Scrap of ¼-inch (6 mm) plywood

Nails or wood screws

Heavy-duty picture hanging hardware

Hooks (optional)

Acrylic paint (optional)

Acrylic medium (optional)*

Container for the paint mixture (optional)

TOOLS

Tape measure or ruler

Pencil

Handsaw

Hammer

Screwdriver

Paintbrush

Sandpaper or sanding sponge

---

* used to thin the acrylic paint

INSTRUCTIONS

1
Measure the inside dimensions of the shutter: the width and height of the slatted part of the shutter, plus 1 inch (2.5 cm) added to the height.

2
Measure, mark, and cut a piece of ¼-inch (6 mm) plywood to the dimensions in step 1.

3
Attach the plywood to the back of the shutter with nails or wood screws.

4
Attach the picture hanging hardware to the plywood.

5
Attach any hardware to the front of the shutter.

6
If your shutter is drab, you can make it more interesting quickly and easily. Simply mix equal amounts of an acrylic color and medium in a container.

7
Add water sparingly to the mixture to create a wash.

8
Paint the shutter with the mixture.

9
Use sandpaper or a sanding sponge to distress the color wash and allow the undercoat to peek out. A light touch is recommended. Allow just as much of the undercoating to appear as you want.

"When you are shopping for your shutter, look around the shop for interesting hardware. The red hooks on this shutter were a serendipitous find that dictated the color that the shutter was painted."

—Terry Taylor

TICK TOCK TIN CLOCK

*O*rnamental pressed ceiling tin makes a wonderful clock face. Designer Jean Moore decided to attach her tin clock to a box made from old bead board to create a novel timepiece.

INSTRUCTIONS

You will be building an open box onto which you will attach the ceiling tin. Using the saw, cut the bead board into two 12-inch (30.5 cm) pieces and two 10-inch (25.4 cm) pieces.

Lay the cut boards on their narrow sides in the form of a box by butting the 10-inch (25.4 cm) boards against the 12-inch (30.5 cm) boards. Use the bar clamps to hold the box together.

Use the try square to make sure the box is square.

Nail the box together, and set aside.

Find the center point of the tin.

Hammer the nail through the center point to mark it.

With the tin face up, drill a hole into the center, wide enough to fit the clock shaft.

Place the tin tile on top of the box, lining up the edges as much as possible. Old tiles are not perfectly square, so compensate where necessary.

Attach the tin to the box with the copper nails. Hammer the nails in at about 1-inch (2.5 cm) intervals around the entire border of the box.

Insert the shaft of the clock movement from the back of the clock through the drilled hole and up into the clock face.

Attach the hands according to the clock movement's instructions.

Paint the cut edges of the bead board with the acrylic paint so that the edges blend in with the original surface of the bead board.

Add detail to the clock by embellishing it with architectural hardware, such as doorknobs, keyholes, etc., attached with small nails.

Timekeeping systems are available in inexpensive, ready-to-go kits. Any craft store will sell you a single, small package that contains everything you need to make your clock run.

DESIGNER
JEAN TOMASO MOORE

MATERIALS

48 inches (12.5 m) of old bead board, 1 x 5 inches (2.5 x 12.7 cm)

Finish nails

8 screws

12-inch (30.5 cm) square of embossed tin ceiling tile

Copper-plated nails, 1 inch (2.5 cm) long

Quartz, battery-operated clock movement with hands

Acrylic paint to match the bead board's color

Hardware embellishments (optional)

TOOLS

Tape measure

Handsaw

2 bar clamps

Try square

Hammer

Drill with assorted bits

Screwdriver

Straightedge ruler

Pencil

Nail

Paintbrush

FIRE SCREEN LIGHT

This accent lighting element looks beautiful set in stone in a garden or embedded in an interior wall. If you can't find a suitable fire screen, use ornate heat registers. Call an electrician to wire the light for you.

1. Find a fireplace screen with cutouts (the fancier the better).

2. For interior applications, a "back box" for the light fixture has to be built. This is a recessed box in a wall that holds the lighting fixture. The size of the box will vary depending on the size of the screen.

3. Once the dimensions of the box are known, hollow out the wall where the screen and box will be placed. The placement must be between two studs.

4. Cut the 2 x 4s to fit as the side of the box.

5. Cut the plywood to fit as the back of the box.

6. Nail the plywood to the 2 x 4s.

7. Create a cutout in the plywood for the light fixture.

8. At this point, an electrician needs to be called in to attach the light fixture to the cutout in the back of the box and the power source.

9. Check to see if the light is functioning.

10. Drill four holes in the grill so it can be attached to the wall. For best results, position the holes so the screws will be fastened to either the 2 x 4s or the studs. Use anchors if necessary.

11. Screw the screen to the wall with the brass screws.

12. Extra trim can be added around the grill's edges to dress it up, if desired.

A halide fluorescent bulb was used for this project. Check local electrical codes and manufacturer tolerances for wattage and heat clearance before starting this project.

DESIGNER
ED DOYLE

MATERIALS

Cast-iron fireplace screen

2 x 4 stock, for sides of box

Plywood, for back of box

Nails

Light fixture

4 brass screws

TOOLS

Tape measure

Pencil

Handsaw

Hammer

Drill with assorted bits

Screwdriver

SALVAGED PICTURE FRAME

With some old, weathered, paint-chipped molding and a simple miter box, you can create vintage frames for your prints or photos that deserve a little extra attention. Or, create unique mirrors that are as good to look at as to look into.

DESIGNER
MOLLY SIEBURG

MATERIALS

Salvaged molding

Wood glue

Molding pins or nails

TOOLS

Straightedge ruler

Pencil

Miter box and backsaw

Fine-grain sandpaper

Belt clamp

Hammer

Nail set

INSTRUCTIONS

1. Decide on the frame's size, and add ⅛ inch (3 mm) to the length of each of the four pieces of the frame for a comfortable fit.

2. Put the molding in the miter box face up, with the recessed side or rabbet (where the picture will eventually sit) toward you.

3. Make a left-hand cut at one end of the molding.

4. Measure and mark the length on the recessed side from the cut that's already been made. Transfer this mark to the face of the molding directly above the recessed side.

5. Make a right-hand cut precisely at the mark you made in step 4.

6. Repeat these steps for the other three pieces. Note: Cut the longer pieces first in case there is a measuring mistake. Then the messed up longer piece could be used as one of the shorter pieces.

7. Clamp the frame to test the fit.

8. Sand the corners without rounding off the edges.

9

Apply a small dab of glue to the ends of the frame. Wipe off any excess glue, and clamp the frame until the glue is dry.

10

Once the frame is dry, lightly hammer in a molding pin at each corner. Larger frames may require several pins at each corner.

11

Use the nail set to countersink the pins.

For a stand-alone frame, drill a hole in the bottom of the frame (on the backside) deep enough to fit in a dowel. The dowel needs to be long enough to keep the frame from falling over. For a secure fit, glue the dowel in place.

Instead of a picture frame, create a unique salvaged mirror.

FLOOR OF YORE COFFEE TABLE

*H*ere's one table you can put your feet up on without being hassled. Hardwood flooring from old-growth trees is stronger and more durable than today's flooring, and used as a tabletop, the wood will look better the more it is used.

INSTRUCTIONS

1 Butt the four 2 x 2s (A, B) to form a box frame.

2 Clamp the frame together, and use the try square to make sure the frame is square.

3 Nail the box together.

4 Nail the plywood (C) to the top of the frame.

5 Glue the four balusters (D) to the plywood in the corners where the frame pieces meet.

6 Clamp the legs to the frame until the glue dries. Or, stand the table up, and lay something heavy on top of the table until the glue dries.

7 Miter each corner of the door casings (E, F) so they fit together.

8 Nail the door casings to the frame.

9 Place the flooring (G) over the plywood, using the tongue and grooves to piece them together. Create a ½-inch (1.3 cm) overhang on all four sides if desired. If the flooring doesn't fit to your satisfaction, cut one of the pieces.

10 Remove an end piece of flooring, apply a thin strip of wood glue to the back, and return it to its location. Repeat with the rest of the flooring.

11 Reposition the flooring, and lay something heavy on the tabletop until the glue is dry.

12 Once the glue is dry, nail the flooring boards along the tabletop ends just before the overhang.

13 Use the nail set to hide the nail heads.

14 Finish the table with linseed oil or polyurethane to seal the wood.

This table measures 15¾ inches (40 cm) high, and the tabletop measures 22 x 50½ inches (56 x 130 cm). Vary the size of this table to fit your needs (or to fit the size of the flooring you have).

"A nice variation could include different kinds of wood flooring scraps glued together to create a unique tabletop."

—*Ed Doyle*

DESIGNER
ED DOYLE

MATERIALS

Finish nails

Wood glue

Linseed oil or polyurethane

WOOD LIST

11 linear feet (3.4 m) of 2 x 2 stock

¾-inch (1.9 cm) plywood, 20 x 48 inches (51 x 120 cm)

4 balusters, approximately 14 inches (35.6 cm) long

12 linear feet (4 m) of ¾ x 2 (1.9 x 5.1 cm) door casing

43 linear feet (13 m) of ¾ x 2½ (1.9 x 6.4 cm) hardwood flooring

TOOLS

Handsaw

2 bar clamps

Try square

Hammer

Miter box and backsaw

Nail set

CUTTING LIST

Code	Description	Qty.	Material	Dimensions
A	Tabletop frame	2	2 x 2 stock	20" (50.8 cm) long
B	Tabletop frame	2	2 x 2 stock	44" (112 cm) long
C	Plywood frame base	1	¾" (1.9 cm)	20 x 48" (50.8 x 122 cm)
D	Baluster legs	4	varies	14" (35.6 cm) long
E	Door casing trim	2	¾ x 2" (1.9 x 5.1 cm)	21½" (54.6 cm) long
F	Door casing trim	2	¾ x 2" (1.9 x 5.1 cm)	49½" (126 cm) long
G	Flooring tabletop	10	¾ x 2½" (1.9 x 6.4 cm)	50½" (126.3 cm) long

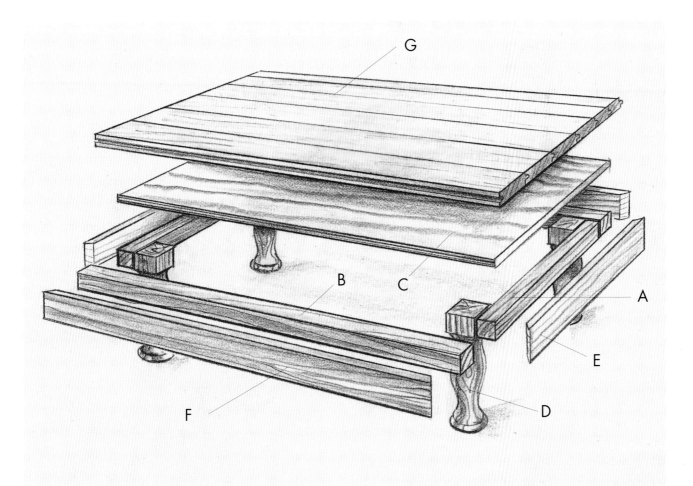

FUNKY MISCELLANY

*T*hough this piece is not functional, it is wonderfully creative. Designer Steve Parker gathered Victorian gingerbread stair spindles, bead board, fencing, rosettes, and more to create this three-dimensional visual collage that seems to float on the wall as if nothing is holding it together.

"In your design, you could incorporate small shelf areas for plants or favorite objects for display that you do not wish to glue to the piece."

—Steve Parker

DESIGNER
STEVE PARKER

MATERIALS

An assortment of architectural fragments

¾-inch (2 cm) plywood scrap for base

Wood glue

Flat-head wood screws (various lengths)

2 heavy-duty eye hooks

Picture frame wire

TOOLS

Screwdriver

2 spring clamps

INSTRUCTIONS

1 Collect salvaged architectural elements that catch your attention. Vary sizes, shapes, and finishes to suit the desired effect.

2 While designing, also consider how each piece will be attached to the pieces below it. In other words, the collage needs to work aesthetically, but it also needs to hold together on the wall.

3 Find or cut a piece of plywood to act as the base. Make sure the base is wide enough to eventually hang the piece, but not so wide as to show.

4 Begin attaching pieces to the base. Screw them on from the back of the

base. Make sure the screws aren't long enough to break through the surface of the elements. Depending on the size, placement, and weight of each piece of wood you are attaching, you may need to have screw attachments in more than one place.

Let the project grow by adding more elements. If you can't screw the piece from the back, use the construction adhesive, and clamp the piece to the assemblage until dry. If you decide to screw a piece to the assemblage from the front, try covering up the screw head attachment with another piece.

Use your judgement as to what will create a structurally sound finished assemblage.

When it is complete, attach the two heavy-duty eye hooks and braided picture frame wire to the back for hanging. Make sure the hanging equipment is designed for the total weight of your assemblage.

COAL GRATE SHELF

This decorative, cast-iron coal grate serves as the base for an elegant shelf that would look fabulous in any room. Some heat registers would also work nicely for this project. The more decorative the grate, the better.

"I was actually looking for an iron gate to make a pot rack, when the person helping us at the salvage warehouse pointed out this grate instead. I put it down, but it was such a striking piece that I came back to it later, thinking it would make a great (no pun intended) shelf."

—Paula Heyes

INSTRUCTIONS

1 Position the board on top of the grate so that the back of the board is flush with the back of the grate.

2 Clamp the board and grate together.

3 Find the best location for the "L" brackets, keeping in mind that the brackets will be holding the shelf together. Mark the placement of the screw holes in the brackets with the pencil.

4 Once the bracket holes have been marked, remove the clamps from the shelf, and clamp the grate to the work surface.

5 Drill the two marked holes where the bracket will be bolted to the grate.

6 Attach the brackets with the bolts using the washers and nuts.

7 Redetermine the placement of the board, and make sure the pencil marks on the bottom of the board still correspond with the bracket holes.

8 Screw the board to the brackets.

9 Along the back of the shelf, attach the flat ring hangers.

DESIGNER
PAULA HEYES

MATERIALS

Coal grate or heat register

Cedar plank or suitable board

2 "L" brackets

2 round head bolts with nuts

2 washers

2 wood screws, size depends on depth of the shelf material

2 small flat ring hangers

TOOLS

2 spring clamps

Colored pencil

Drill with assorted bits

Screwdriver

Wrench

If the grate you find for this project is heavy, hang the shelf from two studs. If that's not possible, use suitable anchors for support.

DISPLAY TABLE

$\mathcal{S}$howcase your collectibles in this weathered table that features a hinged window as both tabletop and display cover. The basic design is so simple that you will have no trouble adapting the instructions for the unique window you find or for the depth of the display you desire.

1. Measure the window frame to get the width and length of the table box.

2. Cut the plywood to the exact outside measurement of the window for the bottom.

3. Cut two barn wood boards the length of the window.

4. Cut two barn wood boards the width of the window minus two thicknesses of the wood. For example, if the width of the window is 19 inches (48 cm), and the width of the wood is 1 inch (2.5 cm), then the length of each of the two boards will be 17 inches (43 cm).

5. Assemble the boards to form a box.

6. Clamp the box, and use the try square to check the box's squareness.

7. Place the window over the box to check the fit.

8. Nail the box together.

9. Nail the plywood to the bottom of the box.

10. Attach the legs to the outside corners of the box with the screws.

11. Screw the hinges to the outside edge of the window.

12. Place the window on top of the table, and screw the hinges to the box.

CANDIS L. KILLAM

MATERIALS

Old window frame with glass

1/4-inch (6 mm) plywood

Old wood such as barn wood*

Nails

Old recycled legs or old wood such as barn wood

Wood screws

2 hinges with screws

TOOLS

Tape measure

Handsaw

Hammer

2 bar clamps

Try square

---

* 1 x 3-inch (2.5 x 7.6 cm) barn wood used for this project

GARDEN BENCH

JOHNNY JONES

*D*esigner Johnny Jones and his 17-year-old daughter, Katina, used an old iron gate, a bed frame, and old bricks to create this unusual bench that makes a stunning garden centerpiece.

MATERIALS

Old gate piece, 36 to 42 inches (91.4 x 107 cm) wide, ideally

9 old bricks

Bed rails

3 scrap metal pieces, the same length as the seat frame

2 angle iron pieces for legs, or extra pieces of gate

TOOLS

Measuring tape

Chalk

Several clamps

Hacksaw

Bandsaw

Framing square

Mig welder

Angle grinder

Sanding pad or wire brush (optional)

Level

1 Place the nine bricks into three rows of three bricks each.

2 Measure the dimensions of the bricks to determine the seat dimensions.

3 With the hacksaw, cut the old bed rails to the dimensions of the bricks.

4 With the hacksaw or bandsaw, miter the corners of the rail pieces.

5 Tack the frame together with the lips turned inward, so the frame will provide a ledge for the bricks along its perimeter.

6 Check the corner angles with the framing square.

7 Check to make sure the bricks fit inside.

8 Weld the frame together.

9 Weld the scrap metal to the inside of the frame at 3-inch (7.6 cm) intervals (to act as braces to keep the bricks in place).

10 Cut the legs so they are the same height. The ideal height of the seat is 16 to 19 inches (40.6 to 48.3 cm) from the ground.

11 Use the angle grinder or sanding pad to clean the tops of the legs.

Weld the legs to the inside front of the seat frame. **12**

Instead of legs, you can cut extra fencing to the desired height of the seat and use the fencing as the legs. Simply weld two fence pieces that match the width of the seat frame to each side of the seat. **13**

Measure the portion of the gate where the seat will be attached. **14**

Clamp the frame to the gate. Check to make sure the seat is level. **15**

Weld the seat frame to the gate wherever the frame touches the gate. **16**

Smooth the welds with the grinder. **17**

Place the bricks in the seat frame. **18**

PEDESTAL

Designer Craig Comeau provides some cool wood-working tricks that make this pedestal a fun and challenging project. Begin by collecting all sorts of salvaged wood you think looks attractive: molding, flooring, trim, barn wood, and even driftwood.

"For me, the materials came first. I started bringing home the antique moldings and hardware from remodeling jobs I was doing. One day I imagined a variety of pedestals for the plants on the floor in front of my bay windows. I already had the materials."

—*Craig Comeau*

TRUNK

1. Cut four trunk sides from the 1 x 10 salvaged wood to the desired length.

2. Miter the trunk sides with the table saw or circular saw so the four sides fit together.

3. Optional: With the jigsaw, create triangular cutouts in each of the four trunk sides that will later accept the trim detail (figure 1 on page 120).

4. Optional: Nail a piece of plywood to the back of the triangular cutouts (figure 1 on page 120).

5. Clamp the four trunk sides together.

6. Measure the inside dimensions of the trunk.

7. Cut eight 2 x 4 blocks to the width of the inside of the trunk.

8. Remove the clamps from the trunk and nail the 2 x 4s in pairs, evenly spaced within two opposing trunk boards (figure 1 on page 120).

9. Glue the two other trunk boards to the trunk.

10. When the glue dries, nail the trunk together and countersink the nails with the nail set.

MATERIALS

Assorted pieces of salvaged wood, molding, and/or flooring

Finish nails

Wood glue

1 x 10 salvaged stock, suggested for trunk

2 x 4 stock, suggested for trunk inserts

¾-inch-thick (1.9 cm) plywood, for base and top

2 x 6 stock, suggested for base triangles

TOOLS

Tape measure

Pencil

Table saw and/or circular saw

Jigsaw (optional)

Hammer

2 bar clamps

Nail set

Bevel square

Miter box with backsaw

Hand planer

1. Determine the desired base size, and cut a piece of plywood to fit.

2. Center the trunk on the plywood and nail it into place.

3. Determine how "thick" you wish the base to be, and cut eight ½-inch-thick (1.3 cm) triangle blocks.

4. Nail the triangle blocks to the base and trunk (figure 1).

5. With the bevel square, determine the angle of the triangle base attachments, and cut desired wood to fit.

6. Miter the wood edges to create a wraparound effect.

7. Nail the trim pieces to the base and blocks. Countersink the nails with the nail set.

8. Repeat with other pieces of collected wood, working upwards until the desired effect is achieved.

Figure 1

TRIANGLE INSERTS (OPTIONAL)

1 Cut the desired molding into eight triangles, which will then be paired up to fit the cutouts at the top of the trunk (figure 1).

2 Glue the pairs together.

3 Plane the edges of each pair, as shown in figure 2.

4 Position the triangles into the cutouts and glue them to the plywood backing.

TOP

1 Wrap the desired trim above the inserts. See figure 2 for one way to place the trim.

2 Determine the size of the top by considering how much lateral flair the selected molding will add to the trunk. The top could extend beyond the molding 1 inch (2.5 cm) all around if desired.

3 Cut a piece of plywood to fit the top.

4 Nail the desired molding to the plywood edges. Countersink the nails with the nail set.

5 Center and nail the top to the trunk.

6 Cut and nail the desired wood for the surface of the top. Old flooring looks nice.

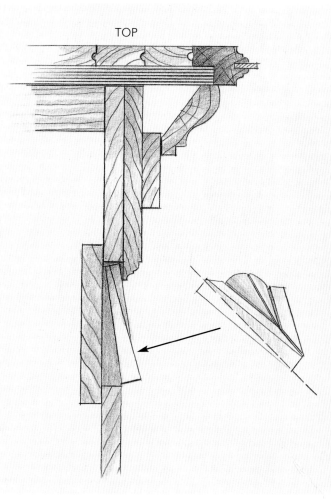

TOP

Figure 2

CURIO CABINET

*D*esigner Will Nicholson salvaged these windows with the original casements from a 1940s farmhouse. This book gave him the perfect excuse to transform them into a beautiful curio cabinet for his wife. He used the whole casement and both window sashes.

1. Remove the inside and outside stops from the casement. Then remove the two window frames. Also remove the inside windowsill and any ropes or weights.

2. Measure the opening in the back, and cut the plywood to fit.

3. Use the try square to make sure the casing is square, and screw the plywood to the back of the casing.

4. Since the length of the casing is too small to fit the window frames into (the windows are made to fit snugly on the sides and overlap at the top and bottom), the bottom window frame will need to be cut (since it has the thickest frame edge). Measure the inside opening of the casement, and then measure the windows. Cut the difference from the bottom window's frame edge. You will probably only need to cut ¼ to 1 inch (6 mm to 2.5 cm) to make the windows fit.

5. If the windows are too wide to fit in the casement, use the hand plane or saw to cut them to size.

6. For the shelves, cut the 1 x 4 stock to fit snugly inside the casing. Make as many shelves as necessary.

DESIGNER
WILL NICHOLSON

MATERIALS

Old double-hung window with casement

¾-inch (1.9 cm) plywood

Wood screws

1 x 4 stock

4 small hinges

2 window locks

2 x 2 stock

TOOLS

Pry bar, chisel, or screwdriver

Tape measure

Circular saw or handsaw

Try square

Screwdriver

Hand plane

Sandpaper

Hammer

Level

Rip the shelves so that the width of the shelves equals the width of the casement minus the width of the windows.

Place the shelves so they will line up with the horizontal window grids.

Once the shelves are in place, check to see they are level, and nail them in through the side of the casing.

Screw two hinges onto each window.

With the cabinet on its back, mount the windows flush with the edge of the casing.

Screw the hinges to the casing.

Screw the window locks to the windows and the casing, making sure they line up.

Cut the 2 x 2 to the width of the cabinet, and nail to the bottom as a base.

WINDOW AND SHUTTER SHOWCASE

The shape and dimensions of the window you find will help determine how you use this display case. A thin, tall window would make a good CD cabinet, while a thick, short window would be perfect for dishes or books.

INSTRUCTIONS

1. Measure and cut the ¼-inch (6 mm) plywood to match the window's dimensions.

2. Screw the plywood to the shutters, forming three sides of a box.

3. Position the window to complete the box, and clamp it.

4. Use the try square to check the box's squareness.

5. Measure the top opening, and cut one of the ½-inch (1.3 cm) plywood boards to fit.

6. Screw the top to the shutter sides.

7. Repeat for the bottom of the box.

8. Remove the clamps and the window.

9. Position the hinges, and screw them to the side of one of the shutters.

10. Lay the box on its back, and attach the window by screwing the other half of the hinges to the window so it swings open. Make sure there is clearance on the bottom so the window doesn't scrape on the floor.

11. Cut the ½ x ¾-inch (1.3 x 1.9 cm) stock into the number of side shelf supports needed. If you have decided on two shelves, you will need four

DESIGNERS

AMANDA DEGELSMITH & MARK BROWN

MATERIALS

¼-inch (6 mm) plywood or other wood

Wood screws

2 shutters, must be the same height as the window

Old window

½-inch (1.3 cm) plywood or other wood

2 hinges

½ x ¾-inch (1.3 x 1.9 cm) stock

1-inch-thick (2.5 cm) board stock

Finish nails

Wood glue (optional)

Doorknob or handle

TOOLS

Tape measure

Handsaw

Screwdriver

2 belt or bar clamps

Try square

Hammer

Level

Drill with assorted bits

supports. The length of the supports should be a few inches shorter than the width of the shutters.

Line up the shelf supports with the windowpanes, make sure the sides are level, and hammer them in on both sides with the finish nails.

Cut the 1-inch-thick (2.5 cm) boards into the number of shelves needed.

Place the boards on the shelf supports. Glue the shelves to the supports if desired.

Decide where to put the doorknob, and drill a hole.

Thread the doorknob screw through the hole and screw it into place.

"We used shutters for the sides because we happened to find a pair that worked, but old barn wood or any other wood will work as well."

—Amanda Degelsmith

NEWEL HOUSE ADDRESS

A newel is a post that terminates the handrail of a stairway at the top or bottom. Designer Terry Taylor wanted to create something with this distinctive post that didn't detract from its natural beauty. He came up with this simple design using scrap copper he had around his house.

1 Remove any loose or unwanted paint from the newel post using a paint scraper or wire brush.

2 Use the awl or permanent marker to trace the outline of the numbers onto the copper sheet.

3 Cut out the numbers with the tin snips or shears.

4 Use the flat file or abrasive sponge to smooth the edges of the numbers and remove small burrs.

5 Use the strips of scrap paper to wrap around the parts of the post where you wish to place the ½ inch-wide (1.3 cm) copper strips as banding. Wrap the paper strip around the post, mark its length with a pencil, and then transfer the measurement to the copper strips.

6 Cut the desired number of copper strips, and set them aside.

7 Place the numbers on the post as desired. Use the awl and hammer to mark the placement for the nails or tacks.

8 Drill small holes through the copper and into the wood with a $\frac{1}{16}$-inch (2 mm) bit.

9 Hammer the copper nails to secure the numbers.

10 Wrap a copper strip around the post as desired. Mark the nail placement with the awl and hammer.

11 Drill through the copper into the wood with a $\frac{1}{16}$-inch (2 mm) bit, and secure the strip with copper nails or tacks. Repeat with the remaining copper strips.

If you feel that your post is not steady enough to stand upright, you can create a base with scrap wood cut larger than the bottom of the post. Simply nail the base to the post and finish as desired.

DESIGNER
TERRY TAYLOR

MATERIALS

Newel post

Stencil or pattern for numerals

Copper flashing or sheet metal

Strips of scrap paper, ½ inch
(1.3 cm) wide

Copper strips, ½ inch
(1.3 cm) wide

Copper nails/tacks

TOOLS

Paint scraper or wire brush

Awl or permanent marker

Tin snips or metal shears

Small flat file or abrasive
sponge

Pencil

Drill with assorted bits

Hammer

GARDEN WINDOW

*U*se this stand-alone window as a garden divider or simply

as a showcase for your favorite garden crop.

INSTRUCTIONS

1 Measure and record the width and height of the window to be used for this project.

2 Rip the boards that will serve as the top and bottom shelves so they are 3 to 5 inches (7.6 to 12.7 cm) longer than the thickness of the window. For example: the window for this project measures 1 inch (2.5 cm) thick, so the top shelf was ripped at 4 inches (10.2 cm), while the bottom shelf was ripped at 6 inches (15.2 cm) wide.

3 Cut the shelves 4 inches (10.2 cm) longer than the width of the window.

4 Rip the two side boards 3 to 4 inches (7.6 to 10.2 cm) wider than the thickness of the window.

5 Cut the side boards 12 inches (30.5 cm) longer than the window (or cut to the size desired).

6 Make sure the side boards are flush with the rear of the top and sides of the window, and nail into place.

7 Center the top and bottom shelves, and nail them into place, making sure they are flush with the back of the window and the back of the side boards, respectively.

8 Paint the boards if so desired.

9 Use the remaining piece of wood to create the sign, unless you already have one.

10 Either stencil or hand paint the sign's "message."

11 Secure the sign under the window with eye hooks or old chain links.

12 To hang the shelf, add picture-hanging hardware to the back.

To convert this from a sign to a planter, simply remove the sign, construct a planter box to your desired specifications, and attach it to the bottom shelf.

DESIGNER
BILL ALEXANDER

MATERIALS

Window

2 pieces of ³⁄₄-inch-thick (1.9 cm) stock, cut 4 inches (10.2 cm) longer than the width of the window

2 pieces of ³⁄₄-inch-thick (1.9 cm) stock, cut 12 inches (30.5 cm) longer than the height of the window

1 piece of ³⁄₄-inch-thick (1.9 cm) stock, cut approximately three-quarters the width of the window (or use an antique sign)

Finish nails

Paint, to match window and for the sign

Eye hooks or old chain links

Picture-hanging hardware (optional)

TOOLS

Tape measure

Pencil

Handsaw

Hammer

Paintbrush

PRESSED TIN SCREEN

𝒟esigner Gail LaMuraglia salvaged the tin for this project from a dilapidated school. For best results, find decorative tin you really like before making final decisions on the height and length of your screen.

INSTRUCTIONS

1. Locate ceiling tin panels that match the size of the screen you wish to create.

2. If necessary, cut the tin panels with the tin snips until they are the same size.

3. Place each panel on the floor and hammer the edges flat, using the wood block as a buffer between the hammer and the tin.

4. Cut the lumber to match the length and width of the tin panels plus ¼ inch (6 mm). In other words, if your tin panels are 36 x 60 inches (92.5 x 152.4 cm), the short rails should be cut to 36¼ inches (93.1 cm), and the long rails should be 60¼ inches (153 cm).

5. Using the dado blade on the table saw, cut a ³⁄₁₆-inch (5 mm) groove down the center of the edge side of the boards that will make the frame. The dado groove should be ¼ inch (6 mm) deep. If you don't have a table saw, use a handsaw to cut the ³⁄₁₆-inch (5 mm) groove, and chisel out the wood carefully to create the groove.

6. Miter the corners of the boards in order to create the frame for the tin.

7. Glue the two long side rails of the frame to the top rail.

8. Use the try square to make sure the corners are square.

9. Clamp the three pieces of wood together until the glue dries.

10. Use the finish nails to further secure the frame.

11. Slide two of the panels back to back into the frame.

12. Glue, nail, and clamp the bottom rail to the side rails, making sure the tin fits in the groove.

13. Repeat these steps for each panel desired.

14. Attach the panels with the hinges and screws.

If you're going to use weathered barn wood, make sure it is structurally sound, since the tin is heavy. You may wish to use 2 x 4s ripped in half, and then add a desired finish. Another solution is to use only one piece of tin for each panel. If you decide to do that, your dado groove doesn't have to be as wide. And make sure the decorative side of the tin is facing out.

DESIGNER
GAIL LAMURAGLIA

MATERIALS

Salvaged barn wood or other wood stock (2 x 2 was used for this project)

Ceiling tin sheets

Wood glue

Finish nails

Hinges

Screws

TOOLS

Tape measure

Tin snips

Hammer

Wood block

Miter box and backsaw

Table saw with dado blade (or handsaw and chisel)

Try square

Clamp

Screwdriver

TIN CANDLE LAMP

*C*reate your own design for these clever little candle lamps, cut from galvanized tin roofing. Designer Bradley Barrett salvaged the roofing shingles for this project from a 110-year-old home.

"I grew tired of seeing houses burned or demolished to make way for newer homes, so against the objections of friends and family I left a job that took me around the world , and began salvaging homes and barns I knew were slated for demolition. Two years later, I had my own architectural warehouse. I love what I do, but the store is secondary. If I could hire an office manager I'd do it in a heartbeat, because I'm happiest out there salvaging."

—*Bradley Barrett*

DESIGNER

BRADLEY BARRETT

MATERIALS

Cardboard

Tape

*11 x 18-inch (28 x 45.7 cm)
galvanized tin roof shingle*

Small nail

Candle

TOOLS

Pencil

Straightedge ruler

Scissors

Tin snips

2 spring clamps

Small chisel

Hammer

Pliers

Figure 2

INSTRUCTIONS

With the ruler and pencil, draw the crosslike pattern seen in figure 1 onto the cardboard.

Cut out the cardboard cross, and tape it to the tin shingle. Use the tin snips to cut out the shape in the tin.

Clamp the tin cross to your work surface, and draw the sun face below, or create your own design, onto the middle of the cross.

Using the chisel and hammer, poke out the design. Fold back the pieces cut out for the design.

With the cross on a flat surface and the longer crosspiece away from you (figure 1), place the ruler where the first ½-inch (1.3 cm) side fold will be made, and, while one hand holds the ruler in place, use your other hand to fold the side piece 90°. Repeat for the rest of the folds noted on figure 1.

Once all the folds are completed, fold the 1¼-inch (3.1 cm) piece of the base of the lamp completely over the 2½-inch (6.4 cm) section (figure 1). Use the pliers to create a flat edge.

Make sure the top piece is covering the ½-inch (1.3 cm) side lips, and fold the ¼-inch (6 mm) lip over the side lips. Use the pliers to create a flat edge, making sure the side lips do not slip out.

Hammer the nail into the center of the base, and place the candle on top of the nail.

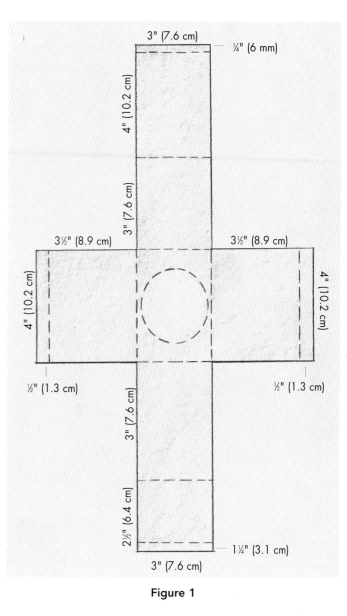

Figure 1

CORNER SHUTTER SHELF

Designer Bill Alexander
put some old bead
board and a matching
pair of shutters to
wonderful use in this
uncomplicated, yet quite
satisfying, shelf.

INSTRUCTIONS

1 Cut the cove molding to the height of the shutters.

2 Form a 90° angle with the shutters, and insert the cove molding into the space created behind the shutters, as shown in figure 1.

3 Check the angle of the shutters with the framing square, and nail the cove molding to each of the shutter frames (figure 1).

4 Measure the inside dimensions of the attached shutters to determine the dimensions of the shelf supports.

5 Cut the 1 x 2 stock to make the shelf supports. Each support will need two pieces that will form a 90° angle.

6 Nail the supports together. Use the framing square to check the angles.

7 Cut and nail pieces of bead board or flooring diagonally to each shelf support. Use the framing square to check the angle of the cuts (figure 1). The finished shelves should fit flush inside the shutters.

8 Space the shelves equally apart, and nail them to the shutter frames.

9 Cut two pieces of bead board or flooring to the height of the shelf for the shelf trim.

10 Nail the bead board or flooring to both sides of the unit.

11 Cut and nail pieces of bead board or flooring diagonally to the top of the shutters. Create a 1-inch (2.5 cm) overhang if desired.

DESIGNER
BILL ALEXANDER

MATERIALS

Piece of cove molding

2 matching shutters 4 to 6 feet (1.2 to 1.8 m) high

Finish nails

1 x 2 stock, for shelf supports

Scraps of bead board or tongue-and-groove flooring

TOOLS

Tape measure

Handsaw

Framing square

Hammer

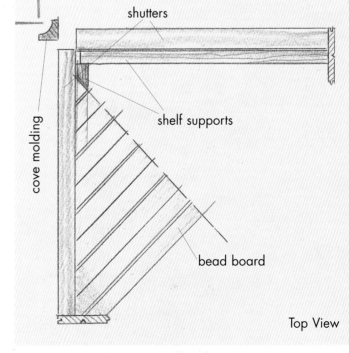

Top View

Figure 1

FENCE PICKET PLANTER

$\mathcal{T}$his planter is a

veritable recycling

center utilizing

balusters, pressed tin,

wooden fence pickets,

doorknobs, and hinges.

"I can imagine using this piece in a bathroom. The box could hold rolled up towels, and the knobs could serve as towel holders. Or, the box could be used to hold books in a garden-themed room. Ah...the possibilities!"

—Jean Moore

1 Lay the picket fence boards on the floor. Arrange them until they please the eye. Try for an overall width of 39 inches (98 cm). This width enables you to create a planter box that will house a standard 36-inch (92.5 cm) rectangular plastic planter insert.

2 Use the framing square to create a straight line at the base of the fence boards. Mark a line across the entire length of the boards with the pencil.

3 Use the saw to cut the boards on the pencil line. Set aside.

4 Construct the planter box.

5 Clamp the box and use the framing square to make sure it is square.

6 Screw the box together.

7 Cut the balusters to the same length, making sure they are even and level. The balusters used in this project were 26 inches (66 cm) long.

8 Measure up from the base of the fence pickets the length of the baluster leg, and use the framing square to draw a line across all the boards. The bottom of the planter box will sit on this line.

MATERIALS

Fence pickets

11 linear feet (3.4 m) of 1 x 9 (2.5 x 23 cm) stock

Wood screws

2 balusters

2 hanger bolts*

2 washers and nuts to fit hanger bolts

2 doorknobs, still attached to the spindle

2 push nuts

Old hinges or other embellishments

Tin ceiling panels

Copper-plated nails, 1 inch long

Approximately 8 feet (240 cm) of chain, ½-inch (1.3 cm) links

2 6-inch (15.2 cm) terra-cotta flowerpots

36-inch (90 cm) plastic planter box insert (optional)

*A hanger bolt has a wood screw on one side and a threaded bolt on the other. This project used 5/16 x 3-inch (8 mm x 7.6 cm) bolts.

TOOLS

CUTTING LIST

Description	Qty.	Material	Dimensions
Front, back, bottom	3	1 x 9" (2.5 x 23 cm)	36" (90 cm) long
Sides	2	1 x 9" (2.5 x 23 cm)	10¾" (27.5 cm) long

9

Position the balusters at the front corners of the planter box. Make a pencil mark on the box where each leg will sit. Drill a hole into the planter box on each side to accommodate the baluster legs.

10

Drill a pilot hole in the center of each baluster top, and use the vise grips to screw the hanger bolts into the holes.

11

Insert the balusters with the hanger bolts through the holes in the planter box, and use washers and nuts to secure them in place.

12

To attach the box to the fence pickets, grab a friend to help you stand the box upright.

13

Line the fence boards up one at a time, line up the base of the box with the pencil line, and screw each board into place.

14

To attach the doorknobs, use the hacksaw to cut the doorknob spindle in half, separating the knobs.

15

Decide on the placement of the knobs, mark the locations, and drill holes into the fence board where indicated.

16

Thread the knobs into the holes, and hammer a push nut onto the back of the spindle piece to secure the knobs.

17

Screw on hinges or any other additional embellishment.

18

Use the tin snips to cut and piece the tin panels together, folding the tin over and under the edges of the box.

19

Hammer the copper nails at 1-inch (2.5 cm) intervals to attach the tin to the box. Use the nicest and most intricate panels for the facade of the planter.

20

To hang the flowerpots, cut the chain to hug the rim at the top of the flowerpot. Use the pliers to open one link, and connect it to form a circle around the pot. Close the link with the pliers.

21

Determine how far down you want the pots to hang, and cut another piece of chain to attach to the chain around each pot.

22

Place the plastic planter box into the planter, if so desired.

TIN
BOX

$\mathcal{D}$epending on the size of the tin you find, this box could serve a variety of purposes. A smaller box would look good on a desk, while larger boxes would make great planters. Before using the box, make sure there are no sharp protruding pieces.

REBEKAH SANDERS

MATERIALS

Paneled decorative tin

2 to 3 tiny screws and bolts

Plywood

Small wood screws

Cork sheeting*

Glue

TOOLS

Tin snips

Needle-nose pliers

Hammer

Nail or awl

Screwdriver

Small wrench

Tape measure

Saw

Pencil

Drill with assorted bits

Scissors

*available at craft stores

1. With the tin snips, cut out a four-panel strip of tin with ½ to 1 inch (1.3 to 2.5 cm) extra on all sides (creating lips for screws), as shown in figure 1. If you have a sheet of tin with three rows of four panels each, you will need to use the middle panels in order to have the extra required to fasten the box together.

2. With the needle-nose pliers, fold and pinch the extra tin on top to create a smooth and even edge (see below).

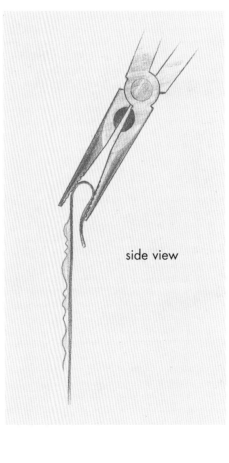

side view

3. With the hammer and awl or nail, punch 3 to 4 holes into each of the side lips, making sure they line up with each other (figure 1).

4. With the pliers, bend the side lips to a 90° angle (figure 1).

5. With the tin snips, cut out triangles on the bottom lip where the panels meet (figure 1).

6. Remove the triangle pieces and bend the bottom lips to a 90° angle.

7. With a hammer and nail or awl, make holes at about 1-inch (2.5 cm) intervals along the base lips. These holes will be used to screw the tin to the plywood base (figure 1).

8. Bend the tin to form the walls of the box.

9. Fasten the box together by putting the tiny screws through the overlapped side lip holes and fasten with the bolts. Tighten with the screwdriver and wrench. If you don't want to use screws, use the needle-nose pliers to fold and pinch the side lips together.

10. Measure the base opening, cut the plywood to fit, and drop it in.

Figure 1

Turn the box over, holding the plywood flush to the bottom.

Using the pencil, mark where the holes in the tin meet the wood.

Drill small pilot holes in the plywood, and then replace the plywood and screw it in. Make sure the screws are the right size so they don't come through the top of the plywood.

Cut the cork with the scissors to fit the bottom of the box, and glue the cork to the base.

CONTRIBUTING DESIGNERS

Bill Alexander specializes in unique, one-of-a-kind, hand-crafted furnishings created from a variety of found and recycled materials including barn wood, windows, doors, shutters, and ladders, as well as branches and twigs. His business, From the Mountains to the Sea, is located in Asheville, North Carolina.

Ivo Ballentine and Robin Cape own and operate one of the largest architectural salvage businesses in the Southeast. Together with their two children, Django and Lucy, they also enjoy building and restoring houses and playing and writing music. Check out their website at www.preservation-hall.com.

Bradley Barrett is a deconstruction specialist and owner of Asheville Recyclers, an architectural salvage warehouse in downtown Asheville, North Carolina.

Mark Brown and Amanda Degelsmith are personal and professional life coaches who help people live richer, more fulfilling lives. In addition, they own a small business called Illumination Inc., in Asheville, North Carolina, where they sell primitive antiques and furniture made from architectural salvage.

Craig Comeau lives with his wife in Asheville, North Carolina. He is a musician, contractor, remodeler, carpenter, tile setter, mosaic artist, furniture maker, and illustrator.

Ed Doyle has been a (self-proclaimed) junk man since 1974. Ed started his business, Mortal Portals, by carving mirrors out of barn wood. He's since gone on to build furniture and houses from Maine to South Carolina (including his own in Burnsville, North Carolina) using architectural salvage.

Suzanne Gustafson is a former physical therapist who now rehabilitates furniture and antiques. Her company is called Bull Creek Designs and Antiques and is located in Asheville, North Carolina.

George Harrison is a custom furniture maker who lives in Weaverville, North Carolina.

Paula Heyes is a talented craftsperson who lives in Asheville, North Carolina with her husband and two sons.

Rolf Holmquist is an artist and printmaker who lives in the cabin he built in Burnsville, North Carolina.

Patti Horton-Blacknight is a former art teacher who has been painting on furniture since childhood. She has sold painted windows in various antique stores, and does custom orders for friends and family.

Dana Irwin is a graphic artist and watercolor painter who lives in Asheville, North Carolina with her three dogs and two cats. She began working with architectural details years ago.

Johnny Lee Jones Is a self-taught furniture refinisher/builder whose store, Classic Antiques (located in Raleigh, North Carolina), has been in business for 21 years. He specializes in architectural iron.

Candis L.Killam combines her creativity and love of gardening and all things old to create a variety of items she makes in her workshop in Asheville, North Carolina, which she markets under the name In the Garden.

Gail LaMuraglia lives in Asheville, North Carolina and displays her work at the Screen Door, a warehouse-turned-shopping experience featuring more than 50 local artists and merchants (many of whom specialize in recycling architectural objects). She attributes her enthusiasm for her work to all things rusty.

Jesse Lee is a woodworker who works extensively with recycled materials. He lives in Asheville, North Carolina.

Josh Malpas is a carpenter whose business is called Beyond Woodland. He lives and works in Asheville, North Carolina.

Jean Tomaso Moore is a part-time multi-media artist who has been creating art in one form or another for as long as she can remember. She lives with her humble and patient husband in Asheville, North Carolina.

Will Nicholson is a woodworker who lives in Marshall, North Carolina with his wife, Melissa, and daughter, Noah.

Steve Parker is the manager of the Screen Door, which houses more than 50 merchants in Asheville, North Carolina. Screen Door offers retail shopping for those seeking the unusual object for their garden, cottage or cabin. At age 16, Steve was already creating metal sculptures from objects he found at various salvage yards and auctions in his home town of Hampton, Virginia. Today, he prefers to work with recycled wooden architectural salvage and offers his creations for sale through his own business, The Green Tire, which is located at the Screen Door.

J. Dabney Peeples is president and senior landscape/garden designer at J. Dabney Peeples Design Associates, Inc., a residential landscape design company located on a 30-acre farm in Easley, South Carolina.

Alan Ruark Is a talented welder plying his trade in Asheville, North Carolina.

Rebekah Sanders is a painter/illustrator who recently graduated from the University of Montevallo in Alabama.

Molly Sieburg has a background in painting and floral design. She currently uses her talents at the Gardener's Cottage, a flower/garden/antique store in Asheville, North Carolina, where she is part-owner, and responsible for most of the buying and all of the displays.

Terry Taylor is an artist who works in many different media and forms. He lives in Asheville, North Carolina.

Joyce Yarling and Roger Leichter retired from careers in jewelry manufacturing and corporate buying, respectively. They married and moved to Asheville, North Carolina to chill out. Their first project was restoring an old house in benign neglect. As the house evolved they found many outlets for their creativity while they personalized their home with their ideas.

Fun with a Miter Saw: Project designer Craig Comeau created this unusual box using both recycled and new molding, topped off with a salvaged doorstop.

ACKNOWLEDGEMENTS

This book is a celebration of the work of 29 very fine craftspeople, artists, carpenters, welders, teachers, salvagers, and others who have graciously lent their talents and projects to this book. Along with the designers, I would also like to thank the following wonderful people for helping to bring this book to fruition:

Bradley Barrett, Asheville Recyclers, Asheville, NC: who let me pilfer through his salvage warehouse and ask a million questions

Ed Doyle, Mortal Portals, Burnsville, NC: for his wit, wisdom, and knowledge

Ivo Ballentine and Robin Cape, Preservation Hall, Asheville, NC: for their input and advice

Kevin Moore and the staff at Olde Good Things in New York, NY: for opening up their digital library to us

Anthony Reeve and Victoria Russell, LASSCo (The London Architectural Salvage and Supply Company), London, England: for providing the photographs seen on pages 6 and 8

Olivier Rollin: for his distinctive illustrations

Sandra Stambaugh: for capturing the perfect shot every time

For their extraordinary help in finding designers and/or projects, I want to thank **Steve Parker, Gail LaMuraglia**, and the staff at The Screen Door in Asheville, NC; **Molly Sieburg** and the staff at The Gardener's Cottage in Asheville, NC; and **Dabney Peeples** and the staff at J. Dabney Peeples Design Associates, Inc.

Dale and Karen Beardsley of Futon Designs, Asheville, NC: for allowing us to borrow the futon sofa mattress and cover seen on page 74

Joanne Ayers, Joyce Yarling, Roger Leichter, Heather Spencer, Charles Murray, and **Robert Todd:** for allowing us to tromp through their homes and gardens in search of perfect photographs

Others to whom I am indebted: **Craig Chenevert, Rebekah Sanders, Terry Taylor, Deborah Morgenthal, Carol Taylor, Rob Pulleyn, Jeff Hamilton, Rosemary Kast, Val Anderson,** and **Caroline Landreth**

And last, I'd like to extend a very special thank you to **Dana Irwin,** who planted the seeds for this book years ago. Her enthusiasm made this book a pleasurable experience from start to finish. She not only designed the book, but also sat through countless brainstorming sessions. Dana's energy is undeniable, and this book is as much hers as it is mine. Thank you, Dana!

INDEX